TO
WALK
WITH
A CHILD

TO WALK WITH A CHILD

Homiletics for Children

A Guide

Gerard A. Pottebaum

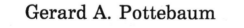

TREEHAUS COMMUNICATIONS, INC. P.O. BOX 249 LOVELAND, OH 45140

SUGGESTED USE OF THIS GUIDE

The questions and suggestions that follow each chapter are intended for group reflection. Parishes may wish to use the chapters of this book as a pre-service or an in-service training program for homilists. Spread over a period of nine weeks, the nine chapters could serve as launching points for nine two-hour sessions.

In so doing, you might start each session with a brief experience of celebrating the word. The scripture texts may be of your own choosing, or drawn from texts referred to in the chapters or complementary to the focus of each chapter.

Following your prayerful reflection on God's word, the structure of your sessions might follow the inquiry method suggested in part three of the book.

First, for about 20 minutes or so, the group members would share what each heard from reading the chapter.

Second, again for about 20 or 30 minutes, the group members might share their reflections on their own experiences that relate to the subject of the chapter. What does the chapter say about our principles and values? This step is one of formulating criteria, standards by which we evaluate our practices.

Third, for another 20 or 30 minutes, the group might focus on the application of those principles. This period might include a reflection on the degree to which your opening celebration of the word embodies the principles you have come to articulate. Moreover, in this part of the session, you may want to formulate actions to take in your celebrations with children. In so doing, you may want to do some specific planning and practicing.

In each phase of a meeting, as in the entire series of gatherings, the underlying agenda is to nurture in members a biblical and childlike spirituality that is as prayerful as it is "practical." By the way, invite and welcome your pastor and other priests.

CHILDREN'S LITURGY CONSULTING SERVICE
(800) 638-4287

You can draw from experience and information gathered over several years from parishes throughout the country by calling the liturgy consulting services provided by Treehaus Communications. Also, through this service, you can be put in touch with other parish leaders willing to share their experience and to learn from your own parish situation. You can also receive information on attending or arranging for workshops and institutes on a variety of subjects, including the spiritual life of children, homiletics for children, liturgy of the word with children, the sacraments of initiation for children, and a variety of other training seminars. Call toll free: (800) 638-4287 between 9 AM and 5 PM Eastern Time.

Library of Congress Catalog No. 93-061738
ISBN 0-929496-95-7
© 1993 Treehaus Communications, Inc.
All rights reserved.

Treehaus Communications, Inc.
P.O. Box 249
Loveland, Ohio 45140-0249
(800) 638-4287

Dedication

Dedicated to the memory of

MARY PERKINS RYAN

*A pioneer and architect
of the modern liturgical and catechetical movements,
mentor and dear friend for many enriching years.*

And to my children's children . . .

ERICA, BRITTANY, *and* BRYAN
ELISE *and* ALLISON
and
MATTHEW
who already enjoys the fullness of God's embrace.

. . . *and to those children still to come.*

*May they all walk hand in hand with joy
to the house of our God.*

Contents

INTRODUCTION

IN THE BEGINNING . . .

We cannot begin anything without starting with what comes first.

In homiletics, what comes first is what is *primal* or *primitive* in us.

But how can we come in touch with what is primitive in us? And why should we want to?

When primitive people gathered around a fire, the fire released more than light and heat. It created its own draft—its own spirit. Primitive people did not sense that presence as they could then see the light and feel the heat of the flames. They experienced it in the wind, in the very same air that gave them breath to breathe. And with that very same breath of the spirit they—*instinctively*—told stories. Like the fire, their stories came together and took on a life unto themselves, through the power of the Spirit. And they became one tribe, one people.

That is what is primitive in us: our instinct to tell stories. Through our stories we come to know the life that is in us and around us—and to share with one another our experience of the Spirit, of the fire within us.

That, too, is what homiletics is about: *our* primal story, the breathing out of God's own life-giving Spirit into God's only-begotten, creative Word. Is this not what the

scriptures tell us God did? In the beginning, God
instinctively spoke. In so many words God said, "Once
upon a time . . . ."
     And time happened.
     That's all it took.
     And it's happening still.
     Out of God's instinctive love.
     Homiletics that reflects this creativity of God begins
with our coming in touch with our primitive *instinctive*
selves. Thereby, we come in touch with that sacred story
through which we realize, that is, we *release* the breath of
the Spirit from within us. That's how God's Spirit moves
in us . . . instinctively.

Not our doing *but our* being

     The challenge in homiletics, therefore, is not one of
learning certain skills, as vital as those may be. The
challenge lies not so much in our *doing* as in our *being*.
This, of course, is a challenge everyone in our society faces.
     We are a society of *doers*. We spend very little time in
touch with simply *being*. However, it is in our *being* that
we find our primitive, instinctive selves, and come in touch
there each with our own "once upon a time. . . ."
     Unlike our primitive ancestors, we no longer gather
around the fire to tell our stories and fail, thereby, to contact
the Spirit. We gather around the television, and let television tell us stories which we are led to believe are our own.
     Television is very seductive. Stories on television
appeal to our basic instincts; however, most really do not
tell our story. Their purpose is not to renew our contact
with mystery and the fire of the Spirit; rather, the stories
of television are designed to control us. Laugh tracks even
tell us when something is—or is supposed to be—funny.
Talk-show hosts and hostesses are skilled at skipping flat
stones between commercial breaks across the troubled
waters of people's lives. Living on the surface, we lose

touch with those deep currents and the "once upon a time" that reveals the meaning of our lives.

So attached to our tubes, what might happen to our society if someone pulled the plug? What would sustain us?

The Fire of the Spirit

We homilists are part of this society; we need to re-establish contact with our primitive human instinct to tell our stories. In doing so, we discover our primal story—that sacred story which carries its own life and power because that story comes from the very breath of God which kindled the original fire of the Spirit in the heart of humanity. That is the fire which draws us together in ritual celebrations.

Homiletics, like television, may appeal to our primitive instincts. Unlike television, however, there is no place in homiletics for exerting control. Nor does homiletics for children have to do with controlling the reactions of children to the story of God's love. We exert unwarranted control, albeit well-intended, when we take it upon ourselves to tell our children what we think they should hear. We control our children when we ask questions that lead them to figure out what is in our heads rather than to reflect upon what God is saying to them in their hearts. Such control smothers the child's instinctive spirit.

Some might express this concern: Does encouraging children's personal responses risk encouraging biblical literalism or fundamentalism? After all, children— particularly young children—tend to take what they hear literally. As some "street-smart" children will tell you, "Step on the crack, break your mother's back." Is it not the homilist's task to make sure our children hear God's word in its proper metaphorical expressions as well as historical settings, so that our children hear what those present in biblical times heard and understood in the original linguistic images?

Moreover, in a related concern, others might wonder: How do our children make the connection between, on the one hand, their personal stories and interpretations of their experiences and, on the other hand, the larger church community story or experience and interpretation of God's presence? Is it not the homilist's task to make sure the children interpret their experiences rightly, that is, in harmony with church teaching?

I hope that in the course of this book such concerns will be addressed, not in the sense that the problems they raise are solved. The homilist, in the course of preparation, deals with the problems presented, for example, by fundamentalism, historicism, pastoral circumstances, exegetics, and so forth. As such, however, the exploration of these matters is more explicitly a concern of catechetics. God's word can be distorted in more ways than we can imagine, not the least of which is listening to God's word through our own digitally-enhanced, laser-sharp societal and cultural biases. While aware of these influences as we guide our children through their reflections on God's word, our primary purpose is *to nurture the assembly's celebration of the mystery of God's presence in the word and to facilitate our children's response in praise, gratitude, and good works.*

Responding to the Spirit

Children have a natural instinct for mystery. Our role as homilists is to encourage children to trust that primal instinct and to share their experiences of mystery through their stories. We do this by the trust we ourselves show in the breath of the Spirit to kindle the stories of our children with the same fire that kindles the primal, sacred story of God's unfailing love. So does each child's story take on the light of God's own "once upon a time" and lead to the church's communal response by which we help to bring God's creation to that time when all people "live happily ever after."

In order to serve this purpose, we have rooted this book in an exploration of the spiritual life of children. That is the focus of the first three chapters. So, too, we have tried to draw the principles of homiletics for children out of the child-like spirituality that is central to Jesus' vision of the reign of God. That is the focus of the middle three chapters. Finally, we arrive at a structured approach to homiletics designed not to control but to guide both homilist and children in listening to God's word, in reflecting on God's word, and in responding to God's word. That is the focus of the last three chapters. (It should be noted that we have not included reflections on integrating the homily with other components related to the Liturgy of the Word—the Responsorial Psalm, Gospel Acclamation, Prayer of the Faithful and Creed. Those matters are treated in this book's companion volume: *A Child Shall Lead Them: A Guide to Celebrating the Word With Children*, published by Treehaus Communications.)

While rooted in the spiritual life of children, this book also attempts to convey a deep concern that goes almost beyond words for our society's insensitivity to our children. This concern is not only for the despicable, criminal abuse so many of our children suffer, but also for the more subtle forms of spiritual abuse visited upon children by our materialistic madness. Surely these are compelling reasons for our children not only to hear the story of God's unfailing love but also to experience that love through *our unconditional embrace*. So, too, is this book an appeal for our children. To those who are hiding the horror of abusing children: What can one say? There's hope . . . seek help. And to all adults whether you have or have not children of your own: All children are *our* children. So, paraphrasing the words of Jesus: Let the children come to you. Bless them . . . not with *things* but with what is *holy* in you. And if you feel you've lost your sense of the sacred, then do yourself a favor: *Walk with a child.*

The Reign of God & the Experience of Children

Throughout the book, we relate the biblical image of
the reign of God to the child's original experience of God's
presence. It is a fitting relationship to draw because Jesus
spoke of children as those who possess the kingdom. In
other words, those to whom the kingdom belongs are those
who experience unconditional love. When food comes to a
hungry person, when shelter comes to a homeless person,
when comfort comes to an abused child, when friendship
comes to those who are lonely, when even the smallest
expression of care comes to any person, without strings
attached, God's kingdom comes. So, too, only when our
hands are empty—when we realize that we have nothing to
offer God in return—can we receive the kingdom . . . and
live happily ever after.

Some readers may wish for hands full of "how-to's"
from this book. Others may look for guidance on such
matters as whether to stand or to sit when reflecting with
children on God's word, whether the use of puppets is
appropriate, or whether children should gather up front
around the homilist or remain in the pews with their
families. Aside from these matters, remember that our
concern is not with our doing, but with *our being.*

Are we real? Are we genuine? That's what we need to
seek: what is in our hearts. There, ultimately, do our
children find the meaning and the mystery in whatever
may be *our doing.*

Everything else follows . . . instinctively.

Gerard A. Pottebaum
The Feast of All Saints

Part One

THE SPIRITUAL LIFE
OF CHILDREN

Chapter One

THE CHILD'S EXPERIENCE OF GOD

"Do you hear what these children are saying?" they asked him.

"Yes," Jesus replied. "Have you never read, 'From the lips of infants and children you have brought forth praise'?"

Matthew 21:6

Why explore, before all else, the spirituality of children in a book on homiletics?

Children play a central role in Jesus' proclamation of the kingdom of God. They enjoy a relationship with God that obligates us in the way we share the word with children. Moreover, the spiritual lives of children provide us with clues to formulate principles and guidelines for the practice of proclaiming the word with children.

In order to appreciate the spirituality of children, ministers of the word may want to explore some of their own childhood experiences of God's presence in their lives. Those experiences profoundly influence the quality and character of our adult spirituality. In our childhood we may not have been very articulate about those experiences.

Robert Coles observes in his book *The Spiritual Life of Children*: "Again and again, children have thought long and hard about who God is, about what God might be like, only to find refuge in the stillness of a room, the stillness of their own minds or souls, as they struggled to express what might well be, for them, the inexpressible."[1] Even as adults, we may find it difficult to describe the presence of God in our lives.

State of Dependence

One quality of the spiritual life of children is their state of dependence. Children depend upon adults for their every need. We do not withhold things from children until they "earn their keep." Moreover, we give children what they need long before they learn to say "thank you." That's the way life is in relation to an ever generous God.

Sometimes we adults forget this. We often lose touch with our dependence upon God. We value *earning* and *deserving* what we receive. We feel obligated to teach this value to our children. However, we adults often tend to emphasize earning one's keep at the expense of nurturing in children gratitude for the gift of life. We forget that with God no one "earns their keep."

But what about each person's need to make a contribution? While making a contribution is a basic component in a person's sense of self-worth, we stand empty-handed before God. Life is a gift from God. When our gratitude—rather than our self-centered desire to earn *our* place with God—moves us to share that life with others, we are an authentic medium of God's self-giving generosity.

It is with empty hands that a child claims food and care from adults. So, too, are we to receive God's kingdom— with empty hands. As we will explore more in a later chapter, Jesus made it quite clear that unless we receive the kingdom as a child receives—with nothing to offer in return—we will not know the reign of God.

From what we have seen so far, we can derive a fundamental principle in the practice of homiletics with children: *the exploration of God's word always reveals God's generous love and ultimately leads toward our expression of thanksgiving.* Moreover, we do not limit our exploration only to biblical texts. In order for our thanksgiving to be more than lip-service—more than an adult prying "thank you" from a child—we also explore the extent to which our lives have been expressions of God's generosity.

In later chapters we will explore the practical ramifications of this principle. At this point, I want only to illustrate how our principles of homiletics arise from and complement the spiritual lives of children.

Sense of Wonder and Awe

When adults report on their early memories of God's presence in their lives, they characteristically describe experiences that have led them to feel wonder and awe. One lady recalled taking nighttime walks with her father on his farm. She remembered holding his strong hand, coarse and calloused from work, as they meandered down a dirt road to a green pasture. There they stretched out on their backs in the meadow grass and gazed at the stars. Small as she was, her imagination sketched enormous creatures in the sky—what her father called "God's own follow-the-dot drawings." There she felt herself in God's own embrace.

Her story prompts me to recall an early grade-school experience of wonder and awe inspired by an elderly, retired Franciscan provincial who visited our classroom to teach religion. While he seemed like a tower to small children, even adults thought of him as a tall, stately man, whose robe flowed with his long stride and whose unfamiliar classic name enhanced his stature. Father Optatus, nevertheless, was a humble man.

His head full of snow-white hair, he used the hood of his fraying habit as a pouch to carry a copy of the Baltimore Catechism. Rarely, however, did he remove or refer to it. He spoke to us not of answers to questions but of matters to ponder.

He wondered aloud in his husky voice about the
mysteries of creation. A man of great size, he stretched
our imaginations with stories about the unfathomable size
of the universe. He counted with us the number of years—
going back before any of us was born—that the light of
certain stars had taken to reach us. He wondered, too, as
we did, about the tiniest of creatures, many too small to
see even under our Cracker Jack magnifying glasses that
so teased our sense of sight and fascinated us.

Although, as children, our knowledge and experience
may be limited, not so our imagination and sense of
wonder and awe.

As the aging and experienced Father Optatus knew, the
power of a child's imagination draws us to the threshold of
knowledge of God. Thereupon, with a child's sense of
wonder and awe can we enter—indeed, we are carried
by the Spirit—into the sanctuary of God's mysterious
presence.

Robert Coles describes still another child's imaginings:
"At only twelve years of age she had learned of His
inscrutability; she had also learned that 'His ways are not
ours.' Though such knowledge was not formally assembled
in her mind, it informed her spiritual life—hence her calm
awareness, a lot of the time, that Jesus is no magician,
switched on by rituals or words. He lives beyond the eyes
and the ears, she told me, beyond the human mind—and
she struggled to bridge that infinite distance with her
imagined scenes, her provocative questions (which could
border on or trespass over to radical doubt). Her wish for
Him to arrive, to take charge of a troubled world, to right
the wrongs she knew existed tells us a good deal about
what was most distinctive about her; but also tells us what
she shared with so many others, a wish somehow to escape
the bounds of the flesh and soar to that place where the
ocean meets the sky, that point of light, that spot in the
infinity of space, where He may well be."[2]

These examples lead us to derive still another principle

of homiletics: *when we share the word with children, we ask them not to echo answers to our questions about God. Rather, we engage their imaginations so that the children can lead us beyond our limited knowledge about God and approach knowledge that is of God, hidden from the wise but revealed to the childlike (Matthew 11:25; Luke 10:21).* Children acquire such knowledge through the grace of imagination, the faculty by which we can fulfill our natural potential for spiritual life and enter with wonder and awe into the presence of God.

Spiritual growth in childhood requires freedom from pre-conceived answers to questions children have not asked. As Edward Robinson observes in *The Language of Mystery*, "Nothing is easier to sentimentalize than childhood. It would be quite wrong simply to identify childhood with creativity . . . as it would be to identify spirituality with the imagination. . . . Childhood, as here conceived, is just another name for that same spiritual potential in each of us. Those who speak of it as something holy are right, but only if they will see it as the seed, the embryo, the root—any of these organic metaphors will do if they remind us that the life that may grow from it is likely to take a shape quite unrecognizable from the form in which we first knew it." [3]

Sensory Knowledge of God

Childhood knowledge of God's presence is characteristically specific and concrete. This knowledge is not the product of abstract thinking. It emerges, instead, from sensory perceptions. In other words, children are able to know God with their whole being, a harmony of heart, mind, and body. This way of knowing complements the knowledge of God that we identify with biblical spirituality.

The knowledge of God that comes to us through the scriptures is vicariously *experiential*—based upon events in the lives of real people through many generations and centuries. These experiences were concrete and specific, just as they are for us today.

The woman who, as a child, felt herself in God's embrace while lying in the meadow with her father under the stars, can still smell the pollen of clover and Queen Ann's lace brushing against her legs, feel grass tickle her arms and neck, hear crickets and croaking frogs in the still of the night. Such an experience of harmony with God rests not on reason or the workings of mind over matter, but on the capacity of one's entire existence to recognize *the presence of the Spirit in matter.*

Although children may not be able to articulate it, this sensory-conscious way of knowing provides children with access, in theological terms, to the mystery of incarnation, the Word of God taking flesh within us.

Here, again, we can derive another principle of homiletics: *when we share the word with children we seek not to draw lessons from the scriptures and apply them to the lives of children; rather, we draw the children inside the scriptures where they will bring with them their own personal experiences and unique awarenesses of being alive.* From that vantage point—from within the scriptures— children tap into their own original sensory-based experiences of God's self-revelation in their lives as they explore the sensory-based biblical way of knowing God. In other words, *we do not conform the scriptures to the lives of children; we invite the children inside the scriptures so that they might conform their lives to God's creative word.*

State of Innocence and Trust

Another way of looking at the spiritual lives of children is from the perspective of innocence which, as we shall see, is related to the child's trust in one's self and others, and, ultimately, in the child's capacity for hope. As developmentalist Erik Erikson points out, "Whosoever says he (sic) has religion must derive a faith from it which is transmitted to infants in the form of basic trust;

whosoever claims that he (sic) does not need religion must derive such basic trust from elsewhere."[4] Obviously, developing basic trust is an affective, intuitive process rather than a cognitive one, and depends upon the attitude of the caregivers who surround the child, beginning in infancy.

When speaking of children's state of innocence, we are particularly at risk in creating an unreal image of childhood. As everyone knows, particularly in our time, children are capable of horrible and cruel behavior. Such cruelty that we hear about in the news, see on television programs, and often witness in our neighborhoods is not what we like to think is natural to childhood.

Perhaps our problem is not with holding childhood up as an ideal state of existence; it is, rather, that we have become callous. Violence and lack of care for one another has become "second nature" to us. We know—or should know—better. Children, however, do not.

Critics of our society observe that we do not let children be children. We expect our children to grow up too soon and with too little personal supervision. We allow almost 90% of our children between 10 and 12 years old to return home from school to empty houses.[5] Our efforts at nurturing are highlighted by athletic programs that—rather than cultivating in children their natural sense of play—put children in fierce competition with each other and inspire unrealistic and self-serving dreams in young children to become multi-millionaire sports heros.

If such insensitivity to the innocence and fragility of children—albeit unintentional—were not enough, we should be aware that we live in a society in which as many as three out of five children are emotionally, physically, or sexually abused. Psychotherapists tell us that children so treated believe something is wrong with them—that they are bad.

What do we expect is happening to the spiritual lives of our children in such a society? Under such conditions, to speak of childhood as a state of innocence is indeed unreal,

a romantic notion. The fact is, however, children do enter
our world in a state of innocence that is of God—but also,
nonetheless, vulnerable to evil. The story of Adam and
Eve in the garden is the classic story of innocence lost.

The innocence of children is fragile. They are open and
receptive—to both good and evil. Children have to be
taught to be suspicious of strangers. Children learn to
trust in others and in themselves through caring adults
who provide a network of opportunities in which children
can equip themselves with inner skills, images, impressions,
and memories that they continue to "check out" against
their outer world. In this process, they correlate their
inner world with their outer world where they, hopefully,
encounter trustworthy people and familiar events and,
thereby, continue to grow in competence. Children who
trust in themselves are able to transcend their limitations
and take new risks with a sense of hope.

In their innocence, children are ready to trust, to
believe. Indeed, their innocence can be interpreted as a
sign of trust and faith in one's self and in others. Unlike
children, adults are like Thomas who—unable to trust—
had to see Jesus' wounds before he would believe. As the
saying goes, "Seeing is believing." Children, on the other
hand, are quite at home "knowing" that when they
believe, then only will they see.

What principle of homiletics can we derive from the
child's innocence and readiness to trust? It is this: *When
sharing the word with children, we must listen with care to
them and fear to challenge what they hear God is saying to
them. Thereby, we nurture their trust in themselves as
dwelling places of God's presence. It is not in what we see,
but in what we believe, that gives us access to the vision of
God's hidden presence.* Our acceptance of the vision of
children enables us to avoid undermining the child's
original state of innocence within which grows the child's
trust of self and sense of self-worth in the eyes of God.
Moreover, when we fail to respect what children have to

tell us about their experiences of God's presence in their lives, we send them a message that conflicts with the biblical teaching that we are each dwelling places of God, temples of the Holy Spirit (*1 Corinthians* 3:16, 17). On the other hand, when we respect our children's experiences, we are teaching our children to respect themselves as the place where God's Spirit dwells.

Sense of Symbol & Ritual

Still another quality of the spiritual lives of children is their capacity to express themselves in ritual. Just as children's experiences of God's presence are concrete and specific, so are their methods of communicating their sense of the sacred.

Children come to know ritual-making through their ordinary experiences. Starting in infancy, children come to know the significance of gesture. The infant learns, for instance, that the outstretched arms of a parent means "come to me," prompting the child to respond excitedly with waving arms and kicking legs.

Family rituals surrounding meals, bedtime, and rising in the morning soon establish for children a sense of security and order. Children are quick to recognize any change at bedtime, for instance, when the Teddy bear is on the left rather than right side of the bed, or if the parent kisses them on the cheek rather than on the forehead, or if a particular prayer has been left out or changed.

Observe the way in which children dress up like adults, or create special environments by arranging large boxes or furniture draped with blankets. Through such symbolic play, children enjoy a sense of managing a world they know to be beyond their control. They recreate the life that embraces them so that they might get to know it better— on their terms.

For children, playing *is* ritual-making . . . so ready are they to encounter the mystery of God's presence and to experience transcendence.

Children receive no training in such ritual play, nor in how to participate in family rites such as birthday celebrations. They learn by doing. Without formal instruction, they know the significance of blowing out the candles—*all* the candles and *in one breath*—after making a secret wish.

The familiar rituals and symbols of our daily lives are integral with the fabric of our spiritual lives. Children are equally at home with both cultural rites and liturgical rites and symbols through which we make tangible the presence of the Spirit of God alive in us. They quickly assimilate the gestures and attitudes of adults at prayer and worship, the postures of praise—and of boredom.

For children, liturgical ritual is "play." As Sofia Cavalletti and others[6] have come to know so well, children readily perceive the sacred character of places and objects and gestures in an environment prepared for prayerful reflection—just as they do when they identify as "sacred" those special places and objects that they set aside in their rooms at home, or that they create outside with cartons and tents or in sandboxes and at beaches. In such settings, notice that even our children's language and manner of expression reveal their awareness of life that transcends the physical evidence of the sacred.

Here again, we can derive a principle of homiletics from children's capacity to ritualize their spirituality. It is this: *When sharing the word with children in "liturgical playtime," ministers of the word are the tangible expression of God's presence to children. So do children sense transcendence in the sounds of our voices and encounter God speaking to them.* We would do well to pause and center ourselves on God's presence in us when we accept this responsibility.

By way of review, we have derived several principles of homiletics from characteristics of the spiritual life of children. Each encourages children to trust in God's unfailing and unconditional love.

- *State of dependence.* Children stand empty-handed before God. So do they possess the Kingdom of God. Our exploration of God's word reveals God's generous love and lead all of us to respond *with gratitude* expressed in praise and in generous love.

- *Sense of wonder and awe.* When reflecting on the word with children, we ask them not to echo answers to our questions about God. Rather, we engage their imaginations so that our children can lead us beyond our limited knowledge *about* God and approach knowledge that is *of* God, hidden from the wise but revealed to the childlike (*Matthew* 11:25; *Luke* 10:21).

- *Sensory knowledge of God.* Rather than drawing (abstracting) lessons from the scriptures and applying them to the lives of children, we draw our children themselves, with their own personal experiences, inside God's creative word. From within the scriptures, children can explore their own original sensory experiences of God's presence in light of God's sensory self-revelation in the scriptures, thereby learning to conform their lives to God's word.

- *State of innocence and trust.* When celebrating the word, we listen with care to our children and hesitate to challenge what they hear God is saying to them. Thereby we nurture their trust in themselves as dwelling places of God's presence. It is not in what we see but in what we *believe* that gives us access to the vision of God's hidden presence.

- *Sense of ritual and symbol.* Playing is ritual-making for children . . . so ready are they to encounter the mystery of God's presence and to experience *transcendence.* When sharing the word with children in "liturgical playtime," ministers of the word are the tangible expression of God's presence to children. So do children sense transcendence in the sounds of our voices and encounter God speaking to them.

These various characteristics of the spiritual life of
children and related principles of homiletics do not,
obviously, exhaust the subject. We are, after all, reflecting
upon the mystery of the movement of the Spirit of God
within our children—and ourselves. Our intent is to
caution those who feel called to share the word with
children: children already have a spiritual relationship
with God. Our respect for that relationship should cause
us to gather humbly with children and encourage them, in
the words of the prophet Isaiah, "to lead (us) to the reign
of God" (*Isaiah* 11:6). So, too, in formulating our
principles of homiletics, we respectfully take direction
from the presence of the Spirit in the hearts of our
children themselves.

Our purpose is not to teach technique, nor is it to
convey 101 ways to make the scriptures come alive for
children. Rather, we want to nurture in ourselves qualities
of childlike spirituality and unclutter ourselves so that we
might acquire the simplicity of holiness.

In other words, if we know not the movement of the
Spirit in our own hearts, how can we proclaim God's word
to others? We cannot give what we ourselves do not have.
So we continue our exploration of childlike spirituality
by focusing now on the spiritual life of children in
the scriptures.

REFLECTIONS

The questions and suggestions that follow each chapter are intended for group reflection. Parishes may wish to use the chapters of this book as a pre-service or an in-service training program for homilists. Spread over a period of nine weeks, the nine chapters could serve as launching points for nine two-hour sessions.

In so doing, you might start each session with a brief experience of celebrating the word. The scripture texts may be of your own choosing, or drawn from texts referred to in the chapters or complementary to the focus of each chapter.

Following your prayerful reflection on God's word, the structure of your sessions might follow the inquiry method suggested in part three of the book.

First, for about 20 minutes or so, the group members would share what each heard from reading the chapter.

Second, again for about 20 or 30 minutes, the group members might share their reflections on their own experiences that relate to the subject of the chapter. What does the chapter say about our principles and values? This step is one of formulating criteria, standards by which we evaluate our practices.

Third, for another 20 or 30 minutes, the group might focus on the application of those principles. This period might include a reflection on the degree to which your opening celebration of the word embodies the principles you have come to articulate. Moreover, in this part of the session, you may want to formulate actions to take in your celebrations with children. In so doing, you may want to do some specific planning and practicing.

In each phase of a meeting, as in the entire series of gatherings, the underlying agenda is to nurture in members a biblical and childlike spirituality that is as prayerful as it is "practical." By the way, invite and welcome your pastor and other priests.

1. Recall one or two of your own childhood memories of what you have come to recognize as God's presence in your life. What circumstances surrounded each experience? What are some characteristics of these experiences? Who was present with you; what part did others play? What was the origin of these experiences; what circumstances brought them about?

2. How do the characteristics of the spiritual life of children described in this chapter complement or conflict with your original experiences of God's presence in your life?

3. What other characteristics of the spiritual life of children can you add to those listed in this chapter?

4. Describe some of your experiences with children that complement the characteristics of childlike spirituality described in this chapter as well as those you have added to those featured in this chapter.

5. Describe in your own words the principles of homiletics that you can draw from the spiritual life of children. Why do you think it is important that our principles of homiletics find their roots in the spiritual lives of our children?

6. Keeping homiletics distinct from catechetics, how do your catechetical programs complement or, on the other hand, have little connection with, the spiritual lives of our children?

FOOTNOTES

[1] Robert Coles, *The Spiritual Life of Children*,
© 1990 by Robert Coles, Houghton Mifflin Company,
Boston, p.168.

[2] *Ibid.*, p.165.

[3] Edward Robinson, *The Language of Mystery*, © 1987 by
Edward Robinson, Trinity Press International,
Philadelphia, p. 82.

[4] Erik Erikson, "Identity and the Life Cycle."
Psychological Issues, Vol. 1. No. 1. © 1959 Random
House/Vintage Books, p. 56.

[5] *CICUPDATE* Newsletter, Volume 3, Number 2, Summer
1992. (Source: "Group," March 1992. Article: "How to
Reach Home-Alone Kids."), © 1992 by Treehaus
Communications, Inc., Loveland, OH 45140, p. 7.

[6] See bibliography for these sources.

Chapter Two

THE SPIRITUAL LIFE
OF CHILDREN
& THE SCRIPTURES

"I tell you the truth, anyone who will not receive the kingdom of God like a little child will never enter it."

Mark 10:15

Jesus gave children a primary place in the kingdom of heaven. Recall when the disciples asked Jesus one day, "Who is the greatest in the kingdom?" In response, "Jesus called a child over, placed it in their midst, and said, 'Amen, I say to you, unless you turn and become like children, you will not enter the kingdom of heaven. Whoever humbles himself like this child is the greatest in the kingdom of heaven. And whoever receives one child such as this in my name receives me' " (*Matthew* 18:1-6).

In order, apparently, to make himself quite clear, Jesus did not stop there. He added: "Whoever causes one of these little ones who believe in me to sin, it would be better for him to have a great millstone hung around his neck and to be drowned in the depths of the sea" (*Matthew* 18:6).

Makes one pause.

Children's relationship with God plays a central role in the message of Jesus. This fact also gives us insight into

Jesus' own spirituality—for surely Jesus practiced what he preached. Aside from his references to children at significant points in his teaching, the way in which Jesus expressed his own relationship to God reveals his childlike spirituality, as Jesus demonstrates, for instance, when he affectionately calls God, "Abba"—in modern idiom, "Daddy."

Although children serve to reveal the core of the gospel, little has been written about children in the Bible. Moreover, the texts on children are more difficult to understand than a superficial reading reveals—more difficult and nuanced than we will be able to uncover here. Our reflections are based largely upon the writing of Joseph A. Grassi and Hans-Ruedi Weber. (See bibliography.) The point we want to emphasize is that Jesus expresses the very heart of the gospel through the way he treats children and speaks about them.

Again, you might ask: Why is it important, in a book about homiletics, to reflect on the place of children in the scriptures? The reasons are several.

Chances are, those of us who are or will be sharing the word with children have been working hard at being *adult* Christians. Our inclination is to figure out how to simplify our adult perceptions so that children can understand what we believe to be an adult religion that they will only fully grasp once they've grown up. This approach is backwards.

The result of such an approach to children—and the gospel—risks abusing the intelligence and depth of spirituality of children. It also results in misusing the scriptures to moralize and admonish children or teach children "lessons" that have little to do with the substance of God's word. For example, using the wedding feast at Cana, where Jesus changes water into wine, as a lesson to teach children to obey their parents, somehow deflates the wonder of that event. It also steals from children a chance to discover, stand in awe, and take delight in who Jesus is.

We cannot share our "adult" spirituality with children

without risking corruption of them. What's more, Jesus
did not tell us to teach children to be like adults. He told
adults to be like children. For this reason, it is important
for those who share God's word with children to become as
children in the biblical sense. As homilists, therefore, we
need to explore the central role children play in the
scriptures and, particularly, in Jesus' communication of
the gospel. With such awareness, we can draw upon the
spirituality of children as a source of grace and guidance in
finding our way to the kingdom of heaven.

This is not to say that we have nothing to offer children.
We do, certainly, have more experience. Children depend
upon us for their physical, emotional, and psychological
support. We are in charge. Moreover, we have a profound
influence as church and as society on the spirituality of
children. If that spirituality is Jesus' standard for entering
the kingdom, does it not stand to reason that we conform
our spiritual lives to that of children in order to be a
mutual source of grace—of knowledge and delight in
God's presence—for the children who gather with us?

Jesus tells us "unless you turn and become like
children, you will not enter the kingdom of heaven"
(*Matthew* 18:3). The message to adults is return to
childhood and start afresh. In this sense, the child is
an image of new life in Christ. Jesus uses this image to
describe conversion and repentance; when you become
like children you are "turning," that is, converting and
repenting from lives that alienate us from God to lives that
admit of total dependence upon God. When Jesus "placed
a child in their midst" (*Matthew* 18:2)—and in our midst as
homilists—Jesus invited us to consider our children as a
significant medium of God's presence. In other words, the
children with whom we gather and, as some would say, the
child within us, offer us an opportunity to return to our
own original childhood experiences of God's presence in
our lives. We homilists have to be humble about who's
converting whom. Unless we become as children, our

children may put on our adult ways. We might ask, "To whose advantage might they put on our ways?"

Recall what Paul told the Corinthians: "When I was a child, I talked like a child, I thought like a child, I reasoned like a child. When I became a man, I put childish ways behind me. For now we see but a poor reflection as in a mirror; then we shall see face to face: now I know in part; but then shall I know fully even as I am fully known" (*1 Corinthians* 13:11-12).

Interpreters of this passage often take Paul's evolving perspective to suggest the superiority of becoming an adult. However, Paul clearly acknowledges that even as an adult he was seeing still only a poor reflection of God's loving presence. Might he also have been revealing a loss of the vision of God children are able to enjoy?

Children & Judaism: God's Blessing

What is the place of children in the Bible and what can we learn from the scriptures about childlike spirituality to which Jesus encourages us adults to aspire?

The Jewish customs recorded in ancient tradition gave children a place of honor, as Joseph A. Grassi points out in his perceptive book *Children's Liberation*. Jewish people believed that children were God's greatest gift to them. When God promised Abram an "exceedingly great reward" (*Genesis* 15:1), Abram was skeptical: "O Lord God, what will you give me, for I continue childless" (*Genesis* 15:2-3). In other words, no material possessions compare with the value of having children.

Later, God took Abraham aside and told him one night, "Look up at the sky and count the stars, if you can. Just so shall your descendants be" (*Genesis* 15:5). Although Abraham was very old, and Sarah his wife was beyond childbearing years, Abraham believed God. Sarah laughed. Nevertheless, how else could Abraham and Sarah fulfill their role as the first parents of the faithful? As a blessing from God, children represented proof of the privilege of

human beings to participate in God's work of creation. "Be
fertile and multiply; fill the earth and subdue it" (*Genesis*
1:27). Later, in Exodus, we find, as Grassi observes: "God
required that the divine origin of this precious gift of life
be especially recognized by the consecration of all first-
born to God: 'To me belongs every first-born male that
opens the womb, all your livestock, whether in the herd
or in the flock.' Then the parents or owners would
symbolically buy them back with a special offering. With
regard to children, the law stated, 'All the first-born
of your sons you shall redeem (*Exodus* 34:20).' "[1]

The ancient people felt strongly that they lived on
through their children. To carry on one's parents' name
was to carry on the life of one's ancestors. A name stood
for the presence of the person. In *Genesis*, for instance,
when Jacob blessed his son Joseph and his grandchildren,
Jacob prayed to God that "in them (the children) may my
name be recalled, and the names of my fathers, Abraham
and Isaac, and they may become teeming multitudes upon
the earth" (48:16).

Because Judaism held children in such high esteem as
God's gift, little wonder that parents sustained the custom
of blessing children. Although mothers sometimes
participated, fathers usually gave the blessing. Noah
blessed Shem & Japheth (*Genesis* 9:26-27). Isaac blessed
Jacob and Esau (*Genesis* 27; 28:1-4). And, as mentioned
earlier, Jacob blessed his children as well as his grandchildren (*Genesis* 48, 49). The significance of receiving the
parental blessing is described in Sirach: "For a father's
blessing gives a family firm roots, but a mother's curse
uproots the growing plant" (3:9).

There is, however, another side to the perception of
children as God's blessing. Parents wanted to make sure
their children grew up to be worthy as God's own gift to
them. Moreover, who wants one's name—one's presence—
to live on in children who have no honor? "He who loves
his son will whip him often," we read in Sirach, "in order

that he may rejoice at the way he turns out" (30:1).

Although the scriptures reveal that children enjoyed a place of honor, we know, too, that parents often treated children badly if not cruelly. While, in practice, the elderly received the most respect, children were expected to obey and respect their parents and elders. Because children were God's own blessing to parents, by obeying and honoring one's parents, children were made to realize they were actually obeying and honoring God.

So the spiritual life of children in the tradition of Judaism was anchored in obeying one's parents as a sign of one's obedience to God—a relationship parents often abused. Even the phrasing of the fourth commandment includes a ramification related to God: "Honor your father and your mother, *that your days may be long in the land which the Lord your God gives you*" (*Exodus* 20:12).

While parents were not sanctioned by law for abusing their God-given children, we read in Exodus: "He who curses his father or his mother shall be put to death" (21:17). Moreover, it was a father's right to sell his daughter. "When a man sells his daughter as a slave, she shall not go free as male slaves do" (*Exodus* 21:7). Grassi observes, "The prejudice of the law in favor of males is blatant, since nowhere does the law allow a son to be sold."[2]

Although we may live in times more enlightened—a matter for reflection in a later chapter—the Israelites were struggling to preserve the Covenant in Graeco-Roman times when children, particularly girls, were considered virtually disposable. The value Israelites placed on children arose from their belief in having been chosen by God to preserve God's will and precepts entrusted to them in the *Torah*. Children were their safeguard to assure their future presence and, moreover, to receive the land that God had promised to them, thus ensuring their presence on earth. In order to make visible their part in the Covenant, infant boys were circumcised. "Thus my

Covenant shall be in your flesh as an everlasting pact"
(*Genesis* 17:13).

Viewed from outside the Covenant and its significance
in the identity of the Israelites, children had no particular
importance, nor did the Israelites idealize childhood.
Before the Babylonian exiles, the Israelites provided no
schools or religious education for children; they learned by
living, working and worshiping with their parents and
families. Later, their education became focused on the
Torah. One learned to read in order to learn the *Torah*.

Children in the Graeco-Roman World

In his book, *Jesus and the Children*, Hans-Ruedi Weber
observes: "In the Graeco-Roman world, children were
generally held in very low esteem. Of course, procreation
was necessary for the continuation of families and nations.
Healthy sons, especially, were valued as future laborers
and soldiers. But children had no worth in themselves,
and their personality was seldom noticed. The Romans
simply gave numbers to their daughters, and their sons
were also given no names from the third or the fifth son
onwards. For a long time, children appeared in Graeco-
Roman art simply as small adults. Thus childhood was
seen as a weak, insignificant, biological state, a preface to
adulthood."[3]

In his review of the place of children in Graeco-Roman
culture, Weber describes the practice of casting out
children considered to be defective. "In Rome, the
new-born child was placed before its father's feet. Unless
the father lifted it up and thus acknowledged the child, it
was exposed. The Latin verb 'to lift up' (*suscipere*) thus
became a synonym for survival. (*Author's note:* "exposed"
children were simply left out in the street or a common
location for someone else to pick up.) Many of the exposed
children died. Others were reared to become slaves. Boys
might be forced to become gladiators while girls became

prostitutes. The elder Seneca, a contemporary of Jesus, reports that in his time professional beggars would collect exposed children, mutilate them and use their misery for begging."[4]

We might observe here briefly that societies have always had to deal with the question of what to do with "unwanted children." In our own society, while it is unlawful to "expose" children, we have pushed the solution to the point of making abortions legal. Whether the unwanted child is "exposed" or "aborted," the fundamental question of how society values a child remains.

The place of children in Graeco-Roman society during the time of Jesus would not be complete without recognizing the emergence of another kind of value placed—albeit ill-conceived—upon children. While less savage, though no less abusive, people conceived of children as play things, purchased at slave markets to serve as sources of amusement, like pets. Children also began to appear in art not as little adults but as chubby little angels, cupids.

Efforts also emerged to reform the otherwise abusive treatment of children in the Roman school system. As Quintilian from Spain wrote approximately 100 A.D.: "He (the child) must be questioned and praised and taught to rejoice when he has done well; sometimes, too, when he refuses instruction, it should be given to some other to excite his envy; at times, also, he must be engaged in competition and should be allowed to believe himself successful more often than not, while he should be encouraged to do his best by such rewards as may appeal to his tender years" (*Institutio Oratoria I*, 1, 20).

Interestingly, during this same time, children were thought to be favored by the gods. Although they shared in the same imperfections as other humans, they were still innocent of adult sexual complications. Their childhood state of purity made the gods look more kindly upon their

requests. Indeed, some children were thought to speak
for the gods, as oracles.

Jesus and the Children

Within the context of the Jewish society and the
Graeco-Roman world, we can better understand the
significance of Jesus' radical view of children. Certainly,
Jesus' evaluation of children was realistic. Recall the
incident in Matthew when John the Baptist sent
messengers to ask Jesus, "Are you the one who is to come
or should we look for another?" Jesus tells them to go and
tell John what they hear and see: people being cured of
every kind of ailment and disfigurement.

Then, after John's messengers leave, Jesus starts
talking about John, identifying him as "the one about
whom it is written: 'Behold, I am sending my messenger
ahead of you; he will prepare your way before you' "
(*Matthew* 11:10). Jesus continues by saying that while
among those born of women there is none greater than
John the Baptist, "yet the least in the kingdom of heaven
is greater than he" (11:11).

Jesus then speaks in a parable about children: "To
what shall I compare this generation? It is like children
who sit in marketplaces and call to one another, 'We played
the flute for you, but you did not dance, we sang a dirge
but you did not mourn.' For John came neither eating nor
drinking, and they said, 'He is possessed by a demon.' The
Son of Man came eating and drinking and they said, 'Look,
he is a glutton and a drunkard, a friend of tax collectors
and sinners.' But wisdom is vindicated by her works"
(11:16-19).

Sometimes, as Jesus must have known, children are
receptive and responsive. At other times they are unable
to get along with anyone, including each other, and cannot
decide about what to do with themselves or with any ideas
someone might have. Jesus used this perception of
children to describe "this generation" of people looking for

the Messiah, particularly the religious leaders. When confronted with the proclamation of the kingdom of God, they rejected the message—both from John and Jesus—like children who prefer to sulk rather than sing, no matter the music (i.e. message), and fail to make up their minds about what to do. In light of the relative utilitarian value Jewish and Graeco-Roman societies placed upon children, Jesus' reference to children served to cut sharply through his listeners' puffy posturing.

Jesus drew upon the lack of regard children received in his time by alluding to children in order to settle an argument among his disciples about who of them would be the greatest in the kingdom. While we referred to this incident at the opening of this chapter, it is worth repeating here as we develop further the place of children in the gospel of Jesus.

" 'If anyone wishes to be first,' Jesus said, 'he shall be the last of all and the servant of all.' Taking a child he placed it in their midst, and putting his arms around it he said to them, 'Whoever receives one child such as this in my name, receives me; and whoever receives me, receives not me but the One who sent me' " (*Mark* 10:35-37).

In this context, the disciple John brings up another argument that had been hanging in the air: "Teacher, we saw someone driving out demons in your name, and we tried to prevent him because he does not follow us" (10: 38). Jesus replied by telling John, in so many words, not to be so controlling and exclusive. We can appreciate Jesus' concern when we observe in our day how denominationalism often breeds such control and exclusivity. We can imagine that Jesus was still thinking about the child on his lap, and about the way children—more so than adults—are ready to accept others, to make playmates with other children whom they do not know. The disciples, on the other hand, still seemed to be preoccupied with authority—who's the "greatest," and who gets to "play their game" with them.

Jesus reveals his awareness of how trusting children are in their willingness to accept others. The disciples' attitude of exclusivity conflicts with Jesus and the spirituality of children. Exclusivity would scandalize children who in their relationships are characteristically inclusive. We can assume that Jesus was well aware how easily someone can dazzle children with "mighty deeds" and then, after winning their trust, give Jesus a bad name and spoil children's trust in Jesus. Jesus would have no part in his disciples' inclination to be exclusive.

Jesus continued to sharpen his point, again alluding to the child in their midst. What's important is not who's doing good things "in my name." The problem is with *pretenders*—those who "perform a mighty deed in my name" and "at the same time speak ill of me. . . . Whoever causes one of these little ones who believe (in me) to sin, it would be better for him if a great millstone were put around his neck and he were thrown into the sea" (*Mark* 9:39, 42).

So precious is the spiritual life of children to Jesus.

The Blessing of Jesus: Inheriting the Kingdom

In his gesture of blessing children, Jesus revealed the central place of children in the kingdom to his Jewish brothers and sisters who, recall, saw children in the context of the Covenant as a blessing from God and a means of assuring their future possession of the promised land. The centrality of children in both acquiring the promised land and acquiring the kingdom of God is striking.

On one such occasion, when people were bringing their children to Jesus to be blessed, the disciples rebuked the parents. "When Jesus saw this he became indignant and said to them, 'Let the children come to me; do not prevent them, for the kingdom of God belongs to such as these. Amen, I say to you, whoever does not accept the kingdom of God like a child will not enter it.' Then he embraced

them and blessed them, placing his hands on them"
(*Mark* 10:13-16).

The scene is reminiscent of the way Simeon embraced
Jesus himself when his parents brought him in infancy to
the temple as was the custom of the law. Simeon blessed
God and prayed in celebration as he held in his embrace
the gift of the kingdom, salvation. Similarly, in his gesture
of embracing the children, Jesus recognized that it was the
children who possess the kingdom. Recall, too, the scene
in *Luke* 15:20 when the father embraced and kissed the
prodigal son, who did nothing to deserve a place in his
father's house.

The question is: how do children merit the kingdom?
None of the texts that refer to children gives any reason.
None ascribe to children innocence or purity or their
capacity to trust, though innocent, pure and trusting they
may be. Jesus' words and gestures reveal not so much the
nature of the spiritual lives of children as they do reveal
the nature of God's love.

No reason is given for why children merit the kingdom
because God's love is "unreasonable." So, too, is it
"unreasonable" for adults to inherit the kingdom. Thank
goodness, God's ways are not our ways.

God's unconditional, gratuitous love which Jesus assured
to the children, turns upside down the Graeco-Roman
value of children and embraces with penetrating clarity
the covenantal value Jewish society placed on children.
Children may be last in the eyes of the world, but they're
first in view of God's kingdom. Whoever wants to enter
the kingdom must look at children in a different way—
seeing how small, dependent, and humble they are. By so
standing before God—small, dependent, humble—will we,
too, be called *blessed . . . children of God* (*Matthew* 5:3-11).

To Become as Children

Of what practical value to homilists are these
reflections on children in the scriptures? Sometimes we

overlook the obvious: *our attitude toward children should be that of Jesus.*

Jesus saw in children the condition of those who possess the kingdom of God. We know that children are dependent, impressionable, and vulnerable, in need of support and gentle guidance, affection, nurturing, stability, compassion, encouragement, comfort, and steadfast protection. In relation to God, Jesus wants us to know, this is everyone's condition. The good news is: God provides for our every need . . . and more.

God's love is beyond reason and imagination and anything that we could earn. We may sell everything we have to purchase the field in which is buried the treasure (*Matthew* 13:44). But the treasure is pure gift—beyond our purchasing power.

We possess the kingdom when we accept the fact that we have nothing to give in return for what God has given us. Then we can rejoice in God's generosity by sharing God's generous love with others: by attending to those who are dependent and vulnerable, in need of support and gentle guidance, affection, nurturing, stability, compassion, encouragement, comfort, and steadfast protection . . . without expecting anything in return.

These are signs of the reign of God happening in our world today. So, too, are the children with whom we, as homilists, gather, a sign of what the reign of God is about. For this reason, it is important that homilists reflect upon the place of children in the gospel and in the vision of Jesus.

Our inclination as adults is to present to children a simplified version of our adult understanding of the message of Jesus. Our children, however, already enjoy a relationship with God that can be for us a source of grace and that can provide us with access to the reign of God. Children do not have to become adults in order to experience the fullness of God's life. However, we adults must become as children to enjoy what God has revealed not to the wise but to those who are like children. So, in Jesus' spirit, we pray, "I give praise to you, Father, Lord of heaven and earth, for although you have hidden these things from the wise and the learned, you have revealed them to the childlike" (*Matthew* 11:25).

Only with this vision, can we be servants of the word.

Summary

As homilists, what guidelines or attitudes can we learn from these reflections on the spiritual lives of children and the scriptures?

• Jesus advises us adults to be like children. Our struggle, as homilists, is *not* to figure out how to simplify our adult perceptions so that children can understand what we believe to be an adult religion that children will grasp once they've grow up. Rather, we ourselves are to embrace the spiritual attitude of children. That is: like children, we stand empty-handed before our God, totally dependent upon God's unfailing love. Only with such childlike spirituality will we enter and be able to invite people into the reign of God.

• The place of children, particularly female children, in the Graeco-Roman and Jewish communities was generally marginal, certainly not central. While the Israelites looked upon children as God's blessing and a means of sustaining the Covenant, their upbringing could be described by today's standards as excessively strict if not at times abusive.

We are also dedicated to passing on our Christian heritage as we struggle to respect the rights of children and to respond with sensitivity to the spiritual lives of children. Homilists play a vital role in communicating our Christian heritage to children. There is no place in that heritage for exclusivity—such as in the treatment of children and women—that often accompanies denomin- ational religion. Those who will be first in the kingdom are those who are as children, that is, those who have no power or place in society or in the institutional church and those who serve the powerless as Jesus served.

• So do we need to stand up for our children and protect them from those societal and ecclesial influences that conflict with the reign of God and steal from children their instinctive knowledge of God's presence. When we respect what children tell us of their experiences of God's presence in their lives, we reflect Jesus' attitude toward children and we verify the message that God has already revealed to them: that they are indeed the place where God dwells (*1 Corinthians* 3:16, 17).

• Jesus' view of children was both realistic and insightful. While the gospel reveals little of the character of the spiritual lives of children, Jesus did hold up the child as a central image in his proclamation of the reign of God. As homilists we might ask ourselves: Does our spirituality reflect that of those who possess the kingdom as Jesus said children do? To what degree are we committed to stand with those who are least among us?

As homilists, we, too, can find access to the kingdom through the children with whom we gather. As servants of the word, we stand humbly with our children, listening with them and to them, seeking through them a childlike vision of the reign of God.

REFLECTIONS

1. What are for you the highlights of this chapter? What parallels might you draw between, on the one hand, the place of children in Jewish and Graeco-Roman society and, on the other hand, the place of children in the institutional church and contemporary society?

2. When Jesus refers to children, what does he reveal of God? In addition to Jesus' references to children, what

do children reveal when they appear in biblical events that surround the life of Jesus?

3. Beyond those mentioned in this chapter, what are some of the ways Jesus revealed a childlike spirituality throughout his life?

4. In what ways is your adult spirituality like that of a child in the biblical sense?

5. How has this chapter influenced your perception of the spiritual life of children?

6. Insofar as homiletics is concerned, explore with others in your group the ramifications of the central role of children in the gospel of Jesus.

7. What are some principles of homiletics that you might apply or an attitude you might adopt based upon the place of children in the life and teachings of Jesus?

FOOTNOTES

[1] Joseph A. Grassi, *Children's Liberation*, © 1991 The Liturgical Press, Collegeville, p. 11-12.

[2] *Ibid.*, p. 18.

[3] Hans-Ruedi Weber, *Jesus and the Children*, © 1979 The World Council of Churches, Geneva, John Knox Press, Atlanta, p. 5-6.

[4] *Ibid.*, p. 6.

Chapter Three

SOCIETY, THE CHURCH, & THE SPIRITUAL LIFE OF CHILDREN

Jesus said to them, "Whoever causes one of these little ones who believe in me to sin, it would be better for that person to have a millstone hung around the neck and to be drowned in the depths of the sea."

(Matthew 18:6)

Society and church profoundly influence the spiritual lives of children, for better or for worse. When we meet with children, we participate in that influence—for better or for worse. We bring with us perceptions and values that we ourselves have adopted, consciously or not, and that influence who we are. We need to be conscious of the baggage and the bouquets we bring with us from the institutional church and society to our children. How does what we bring color our conversations and reflections on the scriptures with children?

In the eyes of our children, homilists are powerful symbolic expressions of God's presence. Parents have heard young children at church whisper in their ears queries about the priest or minister, such as, "When's 'God' going to stop talking?" Ordination matters not; lay homilists carry the same symbolic value for children.

In the child's view, homilists speak with more than usual authority; they represent authority that is of God.

Children do not realize, of course, that we adults bring
with us ecclesial and societal values that are not
necessarily of God. These values and views, by their
association with what children perceive to be "of God,"
take on God's authority.

We bring such influence to bear on our children—
consciously and unconsciously—in the way we treat our
children and communicate with them, whether we gather
with them in separate celebrations of the word or when
children remain in the assembly. For example, when a
homilist gathers children around in front of the assembly
and treats them kindly, calling them by their names,
children will likely feel valued. On the other hand,
children get another message when called from the
assembly more for public display than for recognition and
respect, or to fulfill the self-serving needs of the homilist.

Sometimes assemblies are encouraged to applaud
children, as one does for a performance. For instance,
parishes sometimes applaud children when they return to
their places after gathering up front for a "children's
homily." Why? What message or mixed messages do our
children take from such a response to what is supposed to
be the entire assembly's ritual prayer? Or was the
"homily" actually a little quiz or display of the children's
knowledge of the scriptures? Would we applaud adults in a
similar situation?

In this chapter, we want to explore how society and
church value children and express those values in the way
we treat our children. What are our children learning
from the way we recognize or fail to recognize them in our
liturgical gatherings? Our purpose in these reflections is
to develop greater awareness of our own part in—and
responsibility for—the way our church and society
treats children.

Again, this approach may seem to be taking the long
way to get to the practice of homiletics. However, we need
to try as best we can to stand outside church and society, of

which we are so much a part, in order to examine our use
of the power we have over our children. Recall that Jesus
spent 40 days in the desert before he started preaching.
The desert has a way of purifying those who enter it.
There Jesus struggled with questions of how to use his
power and influence in service of God's kingdom and avoid
the corruptions of earthly kingdoms. In the desert Jesus
saw through the deceptions of self-serving authorities. We
can do the same by standing at a distance—from within the
desert—to reflect on our church and our society in relation
to the spiritual lives of our children.

The Changing Social Value of Children

How would you answer these questions: What is a child
worth? How do you measure a child's worth? What are
your criteria: The emotional fulfillment you receive from
your child? The child's sentimental value? How much it
has cost you to have and raise the child? How much the
child produces of monetary value? How much a child will
be able to produce over a lifetime?

Consider for a moment how you were valued as a child.
Of what value were you to your parents or the significant
adults in your life? How do you think they measured your
worth? By the future security you might provide them?
By the emotional fulfillment you provided them?

The value societies place on children is complex and
varied. In any one society, the educated, wealthy class
tend to value children for reasons that are different from
those held by the working class or the poor. Seen from an
economic point of view, the cost of a child and the family's
income essentially dictate the demand for children. In
addition to economic considerations, our cultural,
religious, and ethnic background influences the way we
value children. It does not serve our purpose here to
explore each of these varied influences. Even in any one
assembly with whom we gather to pray, the children

present there will be valued by their families for a variety of reasons.

It does serve our purpose, however, to put our society's present view of children in an historical perspective, while realizing that our need for brevity risks oversimplification.

The value societies place on children has evolved from century to century. For example, social historians observe that, in the sixteenth, seventeenth, and early eighteenth centuries, particularly in England and Europe, children seemed to hold little emotional value. Parents rarely attended the funerals of their children. Colonial Americans were not indifferent but remained emotionally distant from a child's death.

Over the last 125 years, the value American society placed on children has continued to change. If you had grown up in the working class of the 1800's, you would have been valued for what you could produce in support of your family—as a laborer in coal mines, textile mills, and factories. Similarly, if you lived on a farm, you contributed substantially to the family's survival. Farming parents depended upon having children who would become helping hands. A child's productivity gave insurance companies and the legal establishment a standard by which settlements in the case of a child's accidental or premature death could be determined.

In the nineteenth century, parents were no longer emotionally distant from their children. The loss of a child had become painful. "Traditional parental restraint gave way to unabashed outpouring of sorrow," Viviana A. Zelizer writes in her award-winning work *Pricing the Priceless Child*.[1] While long neglected, children became the focus of attention and American advocates of children sought to reduce infant and child mortality. This new consciousness gave rise in the late 1800s and early 1900s to the founding of the American Pediatric Society, the establishment of the United States Children's Bureau, and legislation that produced heatedly debated child labor laws.

"The child labor conflict is a key to understanding the profound transformation in the economic and sentimental value of children in the early twentieth century," writes sociologist Zelizer. "The price of a useful wage-earning child was directly counterposed to the moral value of an economically useless but emotionally priceless child. In the process, a complex reassessment of children's economic roles took place. It was not just a matter of whether children should work or not. Even the most activist of child labor reformers were unwilling to condemn all types of child work, while their opponents were similarly reluctant to condone all child labor. Instead, their argument centered over conflicting and often ambiguous cultural definitions of what constituted acceptable work for children."[2]

Children in Society Today

As the value of children has evolved in our society during the twentieth century, the economically useless but emotionally priceless child has displaced the useful child of the nineteenth century. In the debate and conflict between the two opposing views, the sacred child won.

Children were not to work for economic gain. Parents were responsible for preparing children for adulthood by protecting, nurturing, and supervising them at home and through schools. Work for children became defined in terms of its educational value. Children worked at home in order to learn moral values and the responsible use of money. Seldom was the work children contributed considered to be of any significance economically. In fact, children received a virtually unearned allowance, although household chores may have been attached, to teach children the value of money and how to be a wise consumer.

As we approach the 21st century, new concerns arise about the value our society is placing on children. We are living at a time when the American dream of owning a home and having children, two cars, and an annual vacation, is becoming an economic nightmare. For growing numbers of married men and women, the dream is impossible unless both partners hold income-producing jobs.

When children enter the picture, parents in growing numbers turn the care of their children over to someone else—grandparents, home-care centers, or large daycare centers. These child care expenses exert even more economic pressure on parents to earn still more money.

Aside from families in which both parents work, a growing number of children are being raised by single parents. For such single-income families, the economic burden and related pressures are compounded. The majority of those who live in poverty in America are children and their mothers. The Census Bureau reports that one in four of the new entrants into the ranks of the poor in the 1980s was under 18 years of age.

It is not unusual to hear those who are educated and financially secure wonder, "Why do people who are poor have so many children?" The question prompts another: "Why do people who are wealthy and able to afford children tend relatively to have fewer of them?" Such questions reveal a mixed bag of values that influence people's decision to have children.

Just how sacred are children in our society? The picture is not pretty. As homilists, we need to be aware of the messages our children are receiving from our society's treatment of them and the feelings of self-worth children bring with them when we gather to reflect with them on their sense of God's presence in—or absence from(?)—their lives.

Whether living in poverty or in plenty, an estimated three out of five children are emotionally, physically, or sexually abused by the significant adults in their lives. The National Committee for the Prevention of Child Abuse verified that reports of child-abuse increased by almost 8% in 1992, continuing a trend that has seen an

increase of 50% since 1985. "The most frequently cited
reasons for higher rates of abuse were economic stress due
to poverty, unemployment and related work concerns."[3]

Children are also visiting violence upon others. During
1992, in the city of Cincinnati, for instance, the number of
children arrested for crimes of violence increased 149% in
one year.[4] The largest arrest increase—82%—was among
13- and 14-year-olds. The number of aggravated assaults,
for example, increased from 93 arrests in 1990 to 265
in 1991.

It may be worth noting that Cincinnati is known as a
conservative, church-going community, predominantly
German Catholic. Also noteworthy, in 1993, "Cincinnati
was named North America's most livable city by the *Places
Rated Almanac*."[5] The statistical measures included
crime, which has not decreased appreciably since 1992,
along with cost of living, job outlook, education, health
care, transportation and so forth. The composite
comparison embraced 343 US and Canadian metropolitan
areas. If the above statistics of crime among children
describes the condition of "North America's most livable
city," we homilists might explore the profile of our
individual cities in order to inform ourselves of the world
as our own neighborhood children experience it.

Societal Influences on the Spiritual Life of Children

The sensitive homilist cannot help but wonder how
the changing values that society has placed on children
influence the individual child's sense of self in relationship
with God. We know from developmental theorists and
social scientists as well as from our own personal experiences
how our images of God are rooted in our human experiences
and, therefore, shaped or mis-shaped by them.

Consider, for example, David Heller's observations,
reported in his book, *The Children's God*, about the
difference between the male and female perceptions of
God as influenced by our society. In his structured

interviews with 20 boys and 20 girls, aged 4 to 12 years,
representing Catholic, Jewish, Protestant (Baptist) and
Hindu religions, David Heller observes: "More specifically
in regard to sex differences, it comes as little surprise that
the boys present such a rational conception (of God). For
the most part, Western society still demands this of males,
renders it functional for them, and rewards them greatly
for accomplishments in rational endeavors. It seems that
even today boys are far more concerned with the affairs
of the state and the rational order of things than, for
example, the affective affairs of the family (McMillan
1982). Thus this age-old socialization phenomenon finds
its way into conceptions of God, God's practices, and
God's way of being."[6]

On the other hand, Heller writes, female children
"describe a deity characterized by aesthetic appeal and by
investment in the artistic world . . . . In general, the God
representations of the girls are not nearly so grounded in
concrete facts and events as are those of the boys."[7] The
female concern with intimacy represents "a knowledge of
the world that is more relational than purely rational . . .
(which suggests that) a strong relational orientation (to
God) results from socialization into the female sex role."[8]

As homilists, we share in these societal influences on
our children's perception of God by the attitudes we
reflect when we gather with children. Are we, for example,
sensitive to the influence of language on children and, in
particular, to the use of inclusive language? What are our
unexpressed expectations of boys and girls?

In addition to Heller's observations from his research,
we can speculate further on the way a society that values
children for what they can produce in economic worth
might influence a child's sense of self in relationship to
God. One could argue that to grow up at such a time in
society might shape a spiritual attitude in children that
leads them to feel they are valued in heaven by God—as
they are valued on earth by societal authority—for what

they can produce. In other words, one earns one's place in heaven as one earns one's place in society.

Who is God in the eyes of the child who is perceived by society as economically useful? On the other hand, who is God in the eyes of the child perceived by society as economically useless but emotionally priceless? The point of these questions does not lie in their answers, whatever one may argue them to be.

Rather, the point is this: Each child's experience of society, ethnic group and culture is unique. Each is an expression of God's presence like none other. As homilists, we enjoy a rare opportunity to validate children's innate experiences of God's presence within them. We do this through ritual-making when, for instance, at the Liturgy of the Word we celebrate God's own creative Word both raising us and rising within us to new life.

Whatever influences society may exert on the child's image of the deity and relationship with God, homilists can facilitate a ritual experience for children that engages their imaginations and frees them from the confining images of God that society's changing value of children visits upon them. We do this by respecting the creative power of God's word, by supporting our children in their reflections on God's word and their explorations of God's way—and, thereby, resisting the impulse to impose upon our children *our* words and *our* ways. Of course, we cannot help but influence children by our words and our ways; that is why our responsibility is to reflect the image of God in our own lives so that as our children grow up under our influence they might grow up in the image of God.

We reflect God's image in the compassion we offer those who suffer, in the hope we offer those in despair, in the love with which we embrace those who are lonely. These are matters not so much of the mind as they are of the heart. If we truly believe that it is God's presence that we celebrate in our liturgies of the word, then we must see to it that our children feel God's compassion, find hope in God's promise of a better life, and companionship in following Jesus' way. In this sense, God's word is *sacrament*. Our children hunger for this experience of holiness. Through the power of ritual, children can grow in awareness of the power of God's presence in their lives.

Ecclesial Influence on the Spiritual Life of Children

We would like to think that our children's experience of church, particularly of its rituals, does nothing but nurture their spiritual lives. Such is not always the case. As the *Directory for Masses With Children* observes: "It cannot be expected that everything in the liturgy will always be intelligible to (children). Nonetheless, we may fear spiritual harm if over the years children repeatedly experience in the Church things that are scarcely comprehensible to them . . ." (Paragraph 2). In fact, as we know, children do experience such conflict and harm.

David Heller singled out several primary tensions that the majority of the children he interviewed felt in the practice of their religions. These include:

• "Concern with the letter and propriety of ritual rather than the spirit in which ritual is performed. . . .

• "The tendency of formal religious teachers and parents to block noninstitutional or unconventional views, and thus to discourage original belief and discovery."[9]

Children desire a more personal and direct experience with God than adult interferences allow. "They seem to feel that such encounters are forbidden; they also harbor much trepidation about foregoing the intercession of adults."[10] When adults are able to protect our children from getting confusing signals from denominational religion, however well-intentioned, that conflict with their childlike experiences of God, our children can enjoy a profound sense of liberation and personal trust in God.

One adult, for example, tells this story: When he was about to make his first communion, the rules of the

church required fasting from all food and drink from
midnight. Without thinking, he took a drink of water
before leaving for church. Thinking he could not make his
first communion, he broke into tears as he told his mother
what he had done. Valuing her child's spiritual needs
above denominational requirements, the boy's mother
embraced him and provided consoling advice that he would
never forget. "Don't worry," she said. "You just go to
communion. The Lord understands." Imagine the relief
this child experienced—and more: this boy came to know
that no denominational regulation is ever to keep the Lord
God from entering a person's life.

All too often, denominational religious practice can
interfere with God's desire to embrace children with
unconditional love. We need to ask ourselves how do our
ritual requirements—wherein we dramatize God's
presence—respect the experience of our children? For
example, as any parent knows, when the neighbor children
are in the yard with something to eat, your child will feel
left out if the neighbor children don't share what they
have with your child. The sharing of food as an expression
of companionship is a profound and meaningful experience
for children.

Consider what children experience in a parish
assembly, for example, when everyone else receives the
bread of the Eucharist and they are refused. From the
viewpoint of the formative influence of ritual, why
shouldn't children share in the table of the Lord,
especially when they begin to feel left out? The point
here is not what might be an appropriate age for children,
or what condition of faith is required to share in the
Eucharist. Rather, the issue is how do our ritual experiences
complement our children's ordinary experiences?

What messages do our children get from our rituals?
Observe the behavior of our children in our ritual
gatherings. How do they show their desire to participate?
How do our rituals acknowledge the presence of our children?

How do we parents relate to our children in our ritual gatherings? How do we adults relate to children who may be next to us? What signs of welcome pass between us?

Within the larger ritual structure, we parents can create our own "sub-rituals" with our children by touching, holding hands, helping our children follow the singing. Although our children may not comprehend the significance of our gathering, they will remember their experience there as one of affection, attention, and care. Only when our assemblies embrace our children will children get the message: You belong.

It is the responsibility of the entire assembly to give our children these experiences to remember of our ritual gatherings. Homilists, however, profoundly influence the tone of the assembly's sense of our children's presence. As the *Directory for Masses With Children* warns, when we fail to include children in our ritual-making, the experience risks "spiritual harm" to children (Paragraph 2). Little wonder that children eventually come to see—and often reject—formal religion as an imposition when our rituals either do not embrace them or are foreign to their experience. Imposed religious practices entrap and smother the spirit.

The Ritual Influence of the Homily

The homily is a significant part of our ritual experience. Our homilies need to recognize the presence of children. The lesson homilists can learn from the formative influence of ritual on our children is clear: *Respect and encourage our children in their innate sense of God's presence in their lives and in their original encounters with God.* Restrain the urge to tell our children what we think they should hear; rather, encourage them to tell what they heard God say to them.

Again, we arrive at a fundamental principle or guideline of homiletics with children: *Listen to our children.* Through our children's own words we have the chance to hear God speak to us with uncluttered simplicity.

As we explore the socialization influence of the church on our children's images of God, we can project what impact women and men who preside at liturgies of the word with children will have on our children's spiritual lives. Obviously, the growing participation of lay people in activities previously performed by ordained male clergy provides an opportunity for children to perceive liturgy as indeed the work of the people. Men and women who are "lay presiders" at parish gatherings have the chance to create new models that communicate to both children and adults a sense of ownership of our church-related rituals and a greater sense of continuity between our rituals and our individual experiences of God's presence in our lives.

Little girls, for example, who see women in the role of presider will find more harmony with an institution that traditionally has excluded women from such functions. Similarly, homilists for children's liturgies of the word can listen to our children with genuine respect. By the way we homilists treat children who gather for liturgies of the word, we can demonstrate our belief that our children already enjoy a spiritual relationship with God. With such an attitude, homilists legitimize children's direct encounters with God in their lives and reduce the tension children feel with the institution's "conventional" views of God.

When we speak of the need to respect what our children tell us about their experiences of God and to interpret for our children institutional teachings and popular conceptions of God, we are ultimately dealing with the most vital component in the spiritual lives of our children—*the establishment of trust.* Children need to know that they can trust what they have come to experience of God.

Nurturing in children a sense of trust in God is an integral part of the parent/child/family relationship. The continuing *trust* that parents and families nurture in children *forms* the foundation upon which a child builds

faith in God. "Trust is not necessarily the first cause of
that faith, owing to the possibility that faith may be caused
by the actual existence of a deity; but trust is the process
which makes it possible for faith to emerge in the child.
By laying the groundwork for stable representations (of
God), trust permits a deity representation to have
consistent meaning in the child's inner world."[11]

Nurturing such trust is a critical concern in our society
wherein growing numbers of children are living in families
under severe economic stress, and suffering from physical,
psychological, and sexual abuse by the significant adults in
their lives. The threatening disintegration of the traditionally nurturing family is taking its toll on the spiritual lives
of our children. These societal conditions demand that
nurturing adults extend themselves beyond caring for
their own children and accept responsibility for creating a
society and church community that embraces all children
with kindness and trustworthy care.

Homiletics vis-a-vis Catechetics

As complex and overwhelming as the needs of our
children may be, parishes face rethinking the assumptions
upon which religious education programs for our children
are based and how well parish structures and resources
serve the spiritual needs of our children. Often parishes
adopt new programs, however, without thinking through
the ramifications of such changes, or we sometimes
unwittingly institute programs that conflict with or cancel
out the effects of one another.

A growing number of parishes, for example, are
adopting so-called lectionary-based catechetical programs.
The change reflects a growing awareness of the formative
influence our rituals have in the initiation of our children.
However, without a strong parish liturgical spirituality
that embraces our children, lectionary-based programs will
only prepare our children in a ritual vacuum.

In our efforts to focus on the lectionary readings, and

in our desire to prepare children so that they "get
something out of the liturgy," we need to take care not to
undermine the efficacy of our liturgical celebration. That
is why, for example, it is important to provide children
with leaflets that contain simply the word of God in
language children can understand, rather than leaflets and
workbooks that focus on what we want children to hear,
often at the expense of inviting the children's responses.

Moreover, we have emphasized the basic homiletic
principle to respect what our children—as church, that is,
the people of God—hear God is saying to them. When our
lectionary-based programs or liturgy-preparation efforts
preempt the liturgical experience by leading our children
to listen, in effect, only for what we tell them to hear
(because we want to make sure they get something out of
the liturgy), we may be spoiling their trust in what they
hear God say to them in their hearts. In other words, sometimes our catechetical efforts, contrary to our intentions,
risk draining power from the nourishing influence of the
homily as a ritual act. Catechetics, in complement with
homiletics, needs to find harmony with our children's
natural spirituality. Catechetics cannot replace or make
up for what is lacking in our homilies and rituals.

Our catechetical processes must teach children to trust
in their original experiences of God's presence in the
lives. Our ritual experience with our children must be
strong enough to feed any pre- or post-ritual reflections or
catechesis. Otherwise we are putting the proverbial horse
before the cart.

Just as our principles and guidelines for homiletics are
drawn from the spiritual lives of our children, so, too,
should our principles and guidelines for catechetics be
drawn. Otherwise one risks canceling out the effects of
the other. Our parish catechetical programs and liturgical
assemblies must embody the awareness that our children
already enjoy a spiritual life that can be a source of grace
for the entire community.

Parishes that demonstrate trust in the Spirit alive in our children embrace not only our children but also the Spirit who dwells in them. The experience of the community's trust nurtures in children the trust they need to have in themselves and in their original experiences of the God whose Son described them as keepers of the kingdom (*Mark* 10:14). Nurturing such trust is a primary function of children's homilists . . . and of children's catechists.

Summary

The ecclesial and societal influences on us as homilists are both subtle and profound. Recognizing when we are people *of the world* rather than people of God *in the world* is a daily challenge. With what awareness, then, can we be worthy servants of God's word when we gather with children?

• As homilists we bring to children our own ecclesial and societal values. We need to keep in mind the difference between *religious experience* which complements the movement of the Spirit in the lives of our children and the *experience of religion* (denominationalism) which may or may not nurture those original experiences of God's presence in our lives.

• Children see homilists as powerful symbolic expressions of God's presence. Children hear in our words more than usual authority. Children can easily be misguided, misinterpret signals, believe what is not so. It is the homilist's responsibility to stand humbly with children before God and to represent and reflect through our humility the presence of a loving and merciful God.

• While church and society continue to influence us, the word of God provides us with the opportunity to see our lives in a new light, under the reign of God. So, when we gather with our children, we, too, listen to God with the anticipation, simplicity, and humility of a child in awe. In this way, we help our children to value God's creative word, to listen to God speak to them in their hearts, to trust in their original experiences of God's presence in their lives, and to enhance those experiences with the vision of the reign of God.

• Homiletics and catechetics that nurture the spiritual lives of children draw their guidelines and principles from the relationship children already enjoy with God, respecting particularly those original peak experiences of God's presence in their lives. As a liturgical, ritual act, homiletics has a primary formative (and, hopefully, nourishing) influence upon children, supported by catechetical experiences that are sensitive to the ritual character of our children's spiritual lives.

In ways such as these, homilists can find in the grace of our children a primary source of renewal for the entire community, so moving us to rejoice and to live—even in our world of false promises—with hope in God's promise of new life.

REFLECTIONS

1. How would you conclude the following sentences?
a. By being present at our church, children learn. . . .
b. Our parish expresses its value of children by. . . .

2. How would you describe some of the positive influences denominational or institutional religion has on the spiritual life of children? Some of the negative influences?

3. How would you complete the following sentences?
a. In our society, our children learn to value. . . .
b. In our home, our children learn to value. . . .

4. In what ways has institutional religion influenced your spiritual life? Positively? Negatively? How has

our society influenced your spiritual life? Positively? Negatively?

5. How would you describe the role of the homilist in light of the profound influence church and society has upon the spiritual life of children?

6. In light of the profound effect that institutional church and society have upon children, how can we awaken in ourselves and in our children the difference between being children *in* the world and children *of* the world?

FOOTNOTES

[1] Viviana A. Zelizer, *Pricing the Priceless Child,* © 1985 Basic Books, Inc., a Division of HarperCollins, p. 25.

[2] *Ibid.*, p 57.

[3] Reported in the *Cincinnati Enquirer*, April 23, 1993.

[4] Reported in the *Cincinnati Enquirer*, May 17, 1992.

[5] Reported in the *Cincinnati Enquirer*, October 26, 1993.

[6] David Heller, *The Children's God,* © 1986 The University of Chicago Press, p. 59. (Clinical psychologist David Heller describes in this book his observations from two-hour, structured interviews with each of 40 children, ages ranging from 4 to 12 years. Twenty boys and 20 girls participated, representing four religions: Catholicism, Judaism, Protestantism (Baptist), and Hinduism (American Ashram Group). Heller describes in detail his method and what we might learn from his limited, though nonetheless significant, research.)

[7] *Ibid.*, p. 66, 67.

[8] *Ibid.*, p. 71.

[9] *Ibid.*, p. 135, 136.

[10] *Ibid.*, p. 134.

[11] *Ibid.*, p. 142.

Part Two

PRINCIPLES OF
HOMILETICS
FOR CHILDREN

Chapter Four

THE ASSEMBLY: MYSTERY OF CHRIST PRESENT

At that time, Jesus, full of joy through the
Holy Spirit, said, "I praise you, Father,
Lord of heaven and earth, because you have
hidden these things from the wise and learned,
and revealed them to little children. Yes, Father,
for this was your good pleasure."

Luke 10:21

Children belong in the Christian assembly. They are as much a part of the Body of Christ as is any other baptized person there. By their participation in the community's ritual gatherings, children are slowly initiated into the life of the community. We can presume that Jesus enjoyed a similar experience of initiation into the Jewish assembly.

Recall the story Luke tells about Mary and Joseph finding Jesus in the temple. It ends the infancy narrative where it began—in the temple. Luke's story conveys the message that Jesus embraced all of Judaism in his teachings and felt very much at home in the temple. "Each year his parents went to Jerusalem for the feast of Passover, and when he was twelve years old, they went up according to festival custom" (*Luke* 2:41, 42). The implication is that Mary and Joseph naturally involved Jesus in this ritual celebration.

The story continues: "After they had completed its days, as they were returning, the boy Jesus remained behind in Jerusalem, but his parents did not know it" (2:41-43). As you know, they thought Jesus was traveling back to Nazareth with friends and relatives. And when they went to find him, he was not in the caravan. So they returned to Jerusalem to look for him.

"After three days they found him in the temple, sitting in the midst of the teachers, listening to them and asking them questions, and all who heard him were astounded at his understanding and his answers" (2:46, 47). What might be the implications of their astonishment? That a boy so young knew so much? If Jesus had indeed spent all three days with the temple teachers, they must have discovered a rich spiritual life in a person so young— although, in Jewish culture, Jesus would soon have been old enough to celebrate his bar mitzvah and enter the adult male community. Moreover, Jesus must have felt quite at home in the temple, in spite of their astonishment at his understanding.

Then, when his parents found him, they were astounded, too. Why? Because they didn't realize how bright Jesus seemed to be? Or was it because Jesus seemed not to realize the worry he had caused them? Or could it be that they did not realize the depth of spirituality children can enjoy?

"His mother said to him, 'Son, why have you done this to us? Your father and I have been looking for you with great anxiety' " (2:48). As any caring mother would have been, Mary was worried. Although nearing his teens, he was, after all, still a child.

"And he said to them, 'Why were you looking for me? Did you not know that I must be in my Father's house?' " (2:49). It may be stretching the point to suggest that Luke wants this story to tell us, in addition to the message that Jesus embraced all of Judaism, that children should feel at home in God's house, or even that children of Jesus' age enjoy a relationship with God. However, recall how Luke ends the story: "And Jesus advanced (in) wisdom and age and favor before God and man (sic)" (2:52).

Of the little we know about Jesus' childhood, that seems to be Luke's repeated conclusion: Jesus grew up, gained wisdom, and lived in God's favor (2:40 & 52). A faithful Jewish boy, Jesus was raised in the religious traditions of his community. Participating in temple feasts and synagogue gatherings was a natural part of his initiation or socialization. So, too, are our liturgical rites and celebrations a natural way of initiating children into the Christian tradition and way of living. It is part of the way we are all—including children—to be about our Father's work.

The Assembly: Temple of the Spirit

One of the fundamental characteristics of the assembly is its formative influence not only upon children but upon all those who gather. The art of ritual-making has not to do with producing "good liturgies"; it has to do with the making of a people.

Rituals reveal who a people are. By their rituals do you know them. Christians are the ones who baptize, proclaim God's word, eat the bread and drink the wine—the Body and Blood of Christ. Recall, early Christians were also known for the way they loved one another.

Liturgical rites are not something we have done to us or for us by others to whom we attribute certain authority. The ritual authority of those who *preside* comes only from the Spirit who already *resides* in the people. God's temple is our own flesh and blood. It is not *we* who move those flesh-filled bones in ritual prayer, nor is it our music, our presiders, or our liturgical movements and manners. It is the *Spirit* within us who moves us to pray.

We do have a choice: we can cooperate or get in the way.

As Father John Ford reminded those who assembled to celebrate the life of Sister Thea Bowman: "If there is no power in the pew, there can be no power in the pulpit. If

there is no Spirit in the pew, there can be no Spirit in
the pulpit."

The role of the homilist is to tap into the presence of
God's Spirit in the people of God—that is, the church—and
thereby to articulate the movement of that loving Spirit
who seeks to awaken in us the glory of God, to heal our
hurting hearts, to walk with us when we're weary, to
strengthen our burden-bent backs, to sustain and draw us
into an even deeper union with the body of Christ crucified
and risen.

Stop and think: What a blessed gift it is to be one who
points to the movement of the Spirit in the tender but no
less troubled hearts of children. Take off your shoes.
Better still, take off all your clothed pretensions. We enter
here holy ground.

Clearly, the liturgical assembly plays the major role in
worship and gives meaning to all other roles. Even the
ordained presider is no more or less than a sign of the
priesthood of the people assembled—including our
children. Moreover, we look to the ordained presider for
those qualities that characterize the spirituality of
children. The priestly people of the assembly is one of the
three major elements in the exercise of homiletics. The
other two are the word of God drawn from the scriptures
and the homilist.[1]

Emphasis is properly placed upon the assembly because
"the church is first and foremost a gathering of those
whom the Lord has called into a covenant of peace with
himself. In this gathering, as in every other, offices and
ministries are necessary, but secondary. The primary
reality is Christ in the assembly, the People of God."[2]

While the reality—that is, the identity—of the
assembly is the body of Christ, there is complex diversity
in this one body. Even in an assembly of children, the
homilist faces a diversity of experiences and expectations.
Children are especially sensitive to individual differences
and, although perhaps not always kind, they are usually

honest and open in their ways of dealing with them, often to the embarrassment of adults.

While quick to notice differences, children are equally facile at finding friends. In so doing, children often look to adults for permission to make friends. Often they come running to us and literally ask us if it's okay to play with another child they've just met. Imagine what it would be like if adults were to come together to form a liturgical assembly with the spirit of children making friends. Until children learn our adult reservations and prejudices, they do not hesitate to play with each other and—until they learn differently—to pray with each other. In this sense, the challenge of the homilist is to give children permission to pray together.

Consider for a moment the ritual character of the way children play. Little girls put on mother's hat or dress and shoes and act out being "mother." They "put on" mother and make her presence—which is beyond their control— felt in themselves. Similarly, little boys dress in clothing to act out their heroes. Moreover, children arrange furniture and blankets and boxes to create worlds that otherwise lie beyond the child's power to control. Such symbolic activity is characteristic not only of children's play but also of ritual prayer, when we dramatize God's presence through the use of ritual robes, sacred symbols, and gestures. So is the spirit of play akin to the movement of the Spirit to pray. This is the Spirit that unites us and moves us to say without hesitation, in Jesus' word, "Abba . . . Daddy."

In order to appreciate the experience, children do not have to talk about the unity of the Spirit they feel in each other. Nor does it heighten their experience to theologize for them about their having been "baptized into the one body of Christ and share in a common faith."[3] Such attempts to deepen the assembly's sense of union with Christ only burden the spirit. The homily is not the place for such academics.

Homiletics is about doing, not lecturing. It's about freeing children of any restraints they may feel to express and share with one another their original encounters with God's presence in their lives.

When we reflect with children on the word, we need to keep in mind that the Word has already taken flesh in their lives. Children will verbalize this experience of God's presence in diverse and, to us adults, illogical ways. It is the role of the homilist to draw upon the diversity of the assembly's experiences and perceptions as a sign of God's universal presence and unconditional love with which God unites and embraces us all. So, too, does the homilist weave these individual perceptions into the fabric of our community's experience of God's love. God leaves no one out. God always forgives and never forgets.

This, ultimately, is the experience with which the homilist, serving as the Lord's host/ess, leaves those assembled: there is a place for everyone at the table of the Lord. Come, have something to eat. "The person who preaches in the context of the liturgical assembly is thus a mediator, representing both the community and the Lord."[4]

The Matter of the Assembly's Size & Composition

Just as the dynamics of a group changes with its size and composition, so is the homiletic experience—that is, ritual prayer—affected by the assembly's size and composition. Consider the wide range of possibilities:

• Large Sunday assemblies of several hundred people, composed of adults and children of all ages, perhaps of several races, a mix of socio-economic levels.

• Small Sunday or weekday assemblies of fewer than 150 people, composed of mixed ages, races, economic (in)stability.

• Weekday gatherings of grade school children, sometimes of one age level, then again of all ages.

• Sunday assemblies wherein children gather in separate liturgies of the word, in groups of fewer than 50 children, ages ranging from 4 years to 12 years.

• Sunday assemblies where more than 50 children—sometimes hundreds—gather for separate liturgies of the word, ages ranging from 2 to 4 or 5 years in some groups; 6 to 9 years in another group; 10 to 12 in still another group; or 2 to 12 years in yet another group.

The possibilities are almost limitless. We cannot attempt to deal with each of the dynamics of each of these assemblies. The principles we will reflect upon, however, cut across all of these possibilities. Their application varies in keeping with each assembly's size and composition. In this chapter, we will limit our focus to some issues related to the place of children in the assembly.

The Place of Children in the Assembly

While everyone may agree that children have a place in God's house, not everyone agrees on just what that place might be. Some, though relatively few, believe children should be seen but not heard—and when heard, removed to a sound-proof room. Others are equally convinced that crying infants are valid voices of praise, as inspiring in their innocence as are trained cantors and choirs in their polished performances.

Some argue that children should remain in the assembly during the Liturgy of the Word. Others argue that most assemblies are inept at including children; therefore, children are better served by separate liturgies of the word, adapted to enable them to hear God's word in language they can understand. These positions give rise to several points of discussion that have ramifications for homilists.

One point is this: having separate celebrations of the word for children should not be motivated by poorly celebrated parish liturgies. The argument is sometimes stated this way: The energy spent on separate celebrations with children should be invested in improving the larger parish assembly's liturgies so that they accommodate the spiritual needs of children as well as of adults.[5]

This argument seems to be based on the assumption that having inclusive liturgies eliminates the need for separate celebrations of the word with children. Why cannot parishes have "good liturgies" for those who remain in the large assembly as well as for those who choose to celebrate the Liturgy of the Word with children in a concurrent but separate liturgical space? Why can't "inclusive liturgies" take on a form that accommodates with liturgical fluidity and grace a separate celebration of the word with children? Such a celebration need not necessarily be initiated in a way that proves to be a "dismissal experience" for children or communicates to children a "second class citizen" status. As some pastors with considerable homiletic skills readily admit, the separate children's Liturgy of the Word makes it possible for them to better serve the needs of the remaining community of faithful.

Current pastoral experience indicates that an estimated 5,000 parishes are holding separate celebrations of the word for children. Such widespread practice attests to the fact that these children generally feel included rather than excluded in the community's ritual. Hopefully, they will benefit from the experience although, from a liturgist's viewpoint, these separate celebrations are often less liturgical than catechetical in their execution. That is a widespread homiletic problem which this book attempts to address.

One may argue that the reason children are enjoying the experience of separate liturgies of the word is because the larger assembly's liturgies are so boring. Is such discomfort reason enough to hold separate liturgies of the word with children? Some would argue "No." However, while poor liturgies may be motivation by default rather than by grand liturgical design, there is good reason to remove children from assemblies that fail to nurture the spiritual lives of children. As the *Directory for Masses With Children* makes clear: "We may fear spiritual harm if over the years children repeatedly experience in the Church things that are scarcely comprehensible to them . . . (Paragraph 2).[6] Consider this image: if your children were caught in a building that is burning because of fire-code violations, would you not rush to remove your children rather than let them burn until the fire is under control and the building brought up to code?

There is no question that the effort to create inclusive liturgical experiences is the goal every parish should strive to achieve. We need not presume that the only way to achieve this goal is by keeping the assembly in one room, fireproof or not.

The Single Assembly as a Norm

Another point of discussion, related to the first one, is about having a single parish liturgical assembly that embraces all people. Obviously, the matter of the assembly's size affects the approach of the homilist. Should the homilist invite the children to gather up front and specifically address them? Or should the homilist address remarks to the children while they remain scattered throughout the assembly? Just what is the place of children in the assembly? What are the ramifications of the arguments some liturgists advance about the place of children?

Some liturgists argue that "most parishes have Masses; few really have an assembly of the local church. Masses are multiplied to meet the demands of numbers or merely for convenience, but the ideal liturgical assembly is a gathering of all God's people in a given place: men, women, children, the elderly, the sick, representatives of every social group and social stratum. This is the church most visible as what she is; the work of Christ, gathering the scattered children of God into one. For most of its history the church resisted the multiplication of Masses. Even as late as the nineteenth century, it would have been thought very odd, on the whole, for most parishes to have more than one Mass, since the Mass by definition had always been understood as primarily the worship offered by the entire people. . . . Suffice it to say that the typical congregation at Mass is not usually an assembly in the full sense of the term."[7]

While it may seem odd to have more than one Mass on weekends, and inconsistent with what used to be the nineteenth century "norm" of a single assembly, the reality homilists face is multiple gatherings of large numbers— whether that's the Saturday evening Mass of those who want to sleep in on Sunday as well as the elderly, single adults, and a scattering of children, or the 10:30 AM Sunday Mass frequented mostly by families with lots of children, or the parish school Mass for kindergarten through upper grades.

Recently a parish built a multi-million-dollar church large enough to accommodate a thousand parishioners. While there was a need for a suitable liturgical space, the reason for building such a large structure was not to reach the ideal of a single assembly. It was, rather, to accommodate the shortage of priests. With the large church, two priests would need to preside at no more than two Masses each weekend.

This may have solved the problem of the clergy, but what of the children in such large gatherings? Carrying this "norm" of the single assembly to the absurd leads one to ask, "Why not rent the local college gym with over 10,000 seats?" That would also solve the priest shortage and one could use the money to build housing for the homeless or more modest spaces for smaller worshiping communities, served by lay people ordained to preside and

share God's word at small, local eucharistic celebrations—
which is not so absurd.

The Spiritual Advantage of Children as a Norm

The *Directory for Masses With Children* both expresses
and implies an over-riding standard that applies here: We
must do what is needed to serve the spiritual advantage of
children. If the large assembly's size gets in the way of
serving the spiritual needs of children, we have the
responsibility to create smaller assemblies wherein
children can enjoy their identity with the life and work
of Jesus.

Separate liturgies of the word with children can serve
this need for smaller assemblies. Such small assemblies,
predominantly but not exclusively children, which gather
for separate celebrations of the word, can then rejoin the
larger assembly for the Liturgy of the Eucharist, thereby
providing the children with a sense of the larger church
without getting lost in the crowd.

Still another point needs reflection that bears directly
upon the spiritual advantage of children. It concerns the
matter of children hearing the word proclaimed in
language they can understand. As Linda Gaupin observes:
"If the motivation for providing separate liturgies of the
word is to help children better 'understand' something of
the life of God or the church, we may be victims of a
mindset that has predominated for several centuries."[8]
"Understanding" is a serious concern for children's
homilists, whether facing a parish assembly of all ages or
one composed mainly of children. The question is, how do
homilists communicate an "understanding" of the
scriptures—particularly when children (and many adults)
have little knowledge of the scriptures?

The Liturgy of the Word with children—or with
adults—is *not* the place to preach with the intent simply to
instruct, although that is what many homilists still do. A
brief introduction to a reading might be appropriate at

times, given to facilitate the hearing of God's word. Even
then, such introductions should not interfere with the
movement of the ritual or be delivered in a didactic
manner.

The purpose of the homilist is to facilitate the
assembly's participation in ritual prayer. The language of
the homilist is poetic rather than didactic, implicit rather
than explicit, experiential rather than expository. The
homilist draws the assembly into the scriptures and trusts
the stories and concrete images of the scriptures—water,
rock, bread, wine, vine, branches, clouds, desert,
mountains, valleys, light, darkness, touch, taste, sight,
blindness, crutches, sheep, clothing, tents—to speak for
themselves of the wonders of our God. This is not to say
that the language of homilists need not be intelligible or
understood by the assembly of children—or adults, for
that matter.

Understanding the Language of Ritual Prayer

Even in ritual prayer—*especially* in ritual prayer—
children need to understand God's word, as adults need to
understand the word, within the context of their own
experience. Otherwise, we might as well return to Latin or
proclaim the scriptures in their original languages. While
the "living word of God cannot be confined or contained"
nor "limited by one's rational comprehension,"[9] God
does indeed speak to us in comprehensible ways and
invites us to respond. That's what language (including
words) is about: communication.

Ritual language reveals and communicates what lies
hidden in our lives—the presence of God with us. This
form of communications also presumes understanding. We
may not be able to comprehend this mystery. Indeed its
presence may even strike us speechless; but we surely can
and do know—through the Word made flesh in us—God's
presence. Without such knowledge, how can we see what
appears not? Or thirst for more . . . as children do naturally?

The problem of the language of homilists with which
we are all too familiar is that it does not communicate an
understanding of the presence of mystery. Rather than
becoming an obstacle, separate liturgies of the word
with children—and a dedicated effort to communicate
with children in the larger assembly—can provide an
opportunity to re-discover that concrete, ritual language
for the spiritual benefit of both children and adults.

There is little doubt that parish assemblies struggle to
achieve in their liturgical gatherings an experience of
worship that embraces infants and elderly and everyone in
between. Underlying these parish struggles is something
more than "what works" or what makes a liturgy "succeed."
The shambles or shinings of our liturgical gatherings
reflect the shambles or shinings of our communities of
faith. This is not to say that those who sing on key enjoy
a greater depth of faith than the tone deaf.

Christian life is more than liturgy. However, our
rituals do reveal who we are and what lies hidden in our
lives. In our liturgies we need to communicate our respect
for each other, our sense of awe and wonder in the
presence of God, and our gratitude for God's unfailing love.
Of what value is it to fill our children's heads with
information about God in educational programs if we
fail in our liturgical assemblies to fill their hearts with
appreciation for God's goodness? What makes a "good
liturgy" is a matter of the heart, how well we show our
appreciation—which is not to say that liturgy is mindless.
Members of the assembly are responsible for facilitating
this awareness in each other, attending particularly to our
children, with the guidance of the homilist.

Liturgy is a labor of love . . . God's labor of love. This is
what the liturgical assembly is ultimately about. This is
what the community of faith gathers to proclaim: our
gratitude for God's saving love. It is the single most
important message homilists highlight in the proclamation
of the word. The assembly itself plays as important

a role as does the homilist in this proclamation.

"We are to be the living gospel. We are to be
the Christian message of good news. We may be the
only gospel that many people will ever read."[10]

Only when there's life in the pew, can there be life in
the preacher.

Summary

We have explored here why the assembly plays the
primary role in our ritual gatherings. Within this context
we have elaborated on the notion that children belong in
the Christian assembly. We have also reflected on some of
the ramifications of recognizing children in the assembly
and how these relate to the role of the homilist.

● Next to the family, the liturgical assembly has a
primary formative influence upon our children. Our
rituals not only reveal who we are, but also form us into a
people. As homilists for children, we play a vital role in
the quality and character of influence our liturgical
gatherings have upon our children.

● The assembly is the temple of the Spirit. When we
enter this temple, we walk on holy ground. The role of the
homilist is to draw upon that presence of God's Spirit in
the people as the primary source of energy that moves us
to give glory to God. Children who gather in our assembly
are a sign of those who already possess the kingdom Jesus
proclaimed.

● The liturgical assembly plays the major role in
worship and gives meaning to all other roles, including
that of the homilist. So do our children play the major
role, whether we gather with them as members of the
larger parish assembly, as separate assemblies of children,
or as assemblies of school children.

● The size and composition of the assembly affects the
way in which homilists serve those gathered and bring the

assembly into focus on God's presence in the word.
Whatever the assembly's size and composition, homilists
have the obligation to include children in our efforts to
celebrate God's presence in the word and to heighten the
assembly's experience of giving praise and thanksgiving to
God with us.

• Sometimes we can serve children more effectively by
inviting them to share in the Liturgy of the Word separate
from the parish assembly. These concurrent gatherings
are not to follow a different ritual, but the same ritual as
the one of the parish assembly, adapted, however, for
children. So, too, these gatherings of children are to be
held in such a way as to recognize and celebrate the
presence of children, and not to make our children feel
any less than full members of the body of Christ.

• In whatever ways we may recognize our children as
full members of the assembly, the overriding principle or
guideline we must follow is to serve the spiritual advantage
of our children.

REFLECTIONS

1. How would you describe the highlights of this
chapter?

2. How would you describe the role of the assembly in
our liturgical gatherings? The role of the homilist in
relation to the assembly?

3. How would you describe the place of children in the
assembly? The formative influence of the assembly on
children?

4. What messages are children getting in our assembly?
In our parish? In our sacramental preparation programs?

5. What messages did you receive as a child from your

assembly? How do these compare with the messages you now receive as an adult? What messages do you want your child to receive?

6. How does this chapter's description of the assembly complement or conflict with your perception of the assembly? Your experience of the assembly in your parish?

7. Under what circumstances do you think it appropriate to have children gather in a separate place for the Liturgy of the Word?

8. How would you describe the importance of having children understand God's word proclaimed in language they can understand? In what sense do children "learn from" the homily? In light of this kind of learning, how does homiletics differ from catechetics?

9. How does your understanding of the role of the assembly affect the way you, as a homilist, relate both to God's word and to the assembly as the body of Christ?

10. The next time you, as a homilist, gather with children, what will you do to relate with greater sensitivity to the mystery of God's presence in the assembly?

FOOTNOTES

[1] *Fulfilled in Your Hearing: The Homily in the Sunday Assembly*, The Bishops' Committee on Priestly Life and Ministry, NCCB, © 1982 United States Catholic Conference, Inc., Washington, D.C., p. 3.

[2] *Ibid.*, p. 4.

[3] *Ibid.*, p. 6.

[4] *Ibid.*, p. 7.

[5] *Children in the Assembly of the Church*, Edited by Eleanor Bernstein, CSJ, and John Brooks-Leonard. "Separate

Liturgies of the Word With Children?" by Linda Gaupin, © 1992 Archdiocese of Chicago: Liturgy Training Publications, p. 72.

[6] *Directory for Masses With Children,* © 1973 United States Conference of Catholic Bishops, No. 2.

[7] *Children in the Assembly of the Church.* "Children in the Assembly of the Church" by Mark Searle, pp. 31, 32.

[8] *Children in the Assembly of the Church.* "Separate Liturgies of the Word with Children?" by Linda Gaupin, p. 70.

[9] *Ibid.*, p. 71.

[10] Steve Mueller, *The Word Made Flesh, Vol. 2 Jesus Christ*, The Treehaus Catechetical Textbooklet Library of Basic Christian Teachings, © 1984 Treehaus Communications, Inc., p. 7.

Chapter Five

THE HOMILIST:
SERVANT OF THE WORD

I have become the servant of the body of Christ, which is the church, by the commission God gave me to present to you the word of God in its fullness.

Colossians 1:25

"Those who humble themselves like this child are the greatest in the kingdom of heaven."

Matthew 18:4

What image comes to mind when you hear the word "homilist?" Chances are you will see an ordained priest or minister. Chances are, too, that you've heard several homilists, some good and others not so good. What would you say are some qualities of a good homilist? Do your qualifications include the person's ability to communicate with children?

Can you recall being in church as a child and listening to a homilist? What is your most vivid memory of your experience? One lady described how she enjoyed the Bible stories and the way they were told.

"The preacher was a very gentle person," she said. "His voice was warm and kind. I felt as if he was talking especially to me."

A man said of his childhood church experience: "I felt ignored."

Still another person recalled: "I don't remember anything the priest said except sometimes he'd talk loud, almost shout. All I remember is standing for the gospel, making the small sign of the cross, watching the priest kiss the book, and then sitting down. I liked sitting. I did not like kneeling with my nose against the pew. I thought they called pews 'pews' because of the way they smelled."

The homilist—and church pews, however understood—can have a significant effect on the child's liturgical experience. The very young child often identifies the homilist as none other than God speaking. For better or for worse, flowing robes and vestments add to the splendor of the image.

The role of the homilist in the Roman Catholic church has traditionally been filled by an ordained priest or deacon. The *Directory for Masses With Children* makes the exception: "With the consent of the pastor or the rector of the church, one of the adults may speak to the children after the gospel, especially if the priest finds it difficult to adapt himself to the mentality of the children" (No. 24). The Directory does not explicitly identify this adult "substitute" as a homilist; nevertheless, that is the service being provided. Those who are called to serve in this way symbolize the dignity of the priesthood which ultimately rests in the people who are the body of Christ.

"The community gathered to worship is a priestly people, men and women (*and children* [author's addition]) called to offer God worship. If this community is conscious of its dignity, then those it calls to service in positions of leadership will be able to recognize their dignity as well. We think of the priest as the representative of Christ. This way of thinking is true, as long as we remember that one represents Christ by representing the church, for the church is the fundamental sacrament of Christ."[1]

When we speak of "homilist" in this chapter and throughout this book, we mean to include the ordained priest and deacon as well as the lay person called to this service. Each enjoys the dignity of the homilist. The occasion may be the parish assembly of children and adults, separate liturgies of the word attended mostly by children, or school assemblies of children. In each setting, the role of homilist is broadly, though no less fundamentally, the same: to facilitate the public prayer of those gathered.

To Praise God With Thanks

When speaking of prayer, we return to a principle described in the first chapter. The homilist's exploration of God's word always reveals God's generous love and ultimately leads toward our expression of thanksgiving. It is with empty hands that God's children—all of us—enter God's kingdom.

"All Christian prayer is thanksgiving," writes Gerard Sloyan. "This is true whether the Lord's Supper is celebrated weekly or not, whether the Greek-derived word, *Eucharist*, is used to describe it or not. We assemble in a spirit of thanks for all that the Lord has done for us. But we cannot know what to be thankful for on this Sunday morning unless the word of God has stirred up in us remembrance of the divine goodness. That is true whether the gift of God be centuries old or a matter of the last few days. . . . That is why the scriptures are first read out and commented on: to situate us not in ancient Israel, the shore of Genesareth, or the diaspora of Paul, but in the presence of God in our own setting—where we are 'before the Lord.' "[2]

As we stand "before the Lord" with empty hands, our hearts are full of gratitude. We explore God's word in order to remind ourselves again why we must join heart with voice to proclaim our thanks and give glory to God. Give thanks we must.

"First, effective exploration of God's word without the opportunity to give thanks in symbolic act is a cruel abortment. Second, the call to such an act when our own lives have not been explored, only those of biblical prophets and apostles, is an exercise in religious imagination. The first says: You have examined all the reasons to express your thankfulness, but why bother? The second says: Be thankful blindly without considering in your hearts why. Neither position is satisfactory for a people that has accepted the challenge of addressing God through Christ in terms of affection and awe. In Zen you can hear the sound of one hand clapping. Christian hands are two. There is no effective word without sacrament, no effective sacrament without word."[3]

The Homilist as Prayerful Servant of the Word

The role of the homilist is to help children recognize in their lives the goodness of God. The homilist does this not on the homilist's authority, but on the authority of God's word. The "good" homilist, therefore, is preoccupied not with conveying one's own knowledge of the scriptures, but with being a prayerful servant of the word. As servant, the homilist walks with children by following their lead, listening with them and to them with wonder and awe as they share with us their original experiences of God's presence in their lives.

The *listening skills* of the homilist include the ability to empathize with children, to identify with their feelings of sadness and joy, despair and delight. The homilist tries to read the implications of what children tell about their lives, especially when their reflections seem totally unconnected to the scripture readings or unrelated to the train of the assembly's thoughts.

One Sunday morning, a homilist was reflecting on the story of Emmaus with a small group of children in a separate Liturgy of the Word. Out of the blue, one child announced, "We went to the zoo yesterday." Not knowing how a visit to the zoo might relate to Emmaus, the homilist asked, "Would you like to tell us more about that?" As the child's story unfolded, she told about their family meeting and making friends with a lone, elderly man there who joined them for lunch. "He told us all

kinds of exciting stories," she said. "Then he left." Later,
when they looked for the man to say goodbye, they
couldn't find him. Aside from the obvious connections,
who knows how deep was this child's sense of Christ's
presence in what was to her a memorable and even
mysterious encounter.

Moreover, the homilist tries to read the faces of
children, and to respect what they might be hearing with
their hearts in the sounds of their silence. In one
gathering of children, an older boy, about 11 years of age,
always took the same place, leaning quietly against the
wall in the back of the children's chapel. The homilist
allowed him his space and his quiet. She exerted no
influence on him to contribute his reflections to the
gathering. Then one day, as the group was returning to
the main assembly, the boy waited until last to walk next
to the homilist. He took her arm to draw her near and
whispered, "I like coming here." Then, pointing to his
chest, he said, "It makes me feel good in here."

The *storytelling skills* of the homilist include the
ability to engage the imagination of children. Imagination
provides access to the mystery of life in Christ. Week
after week, the homilist invites children to discover the
harmony between their lives and life in Christ. The
homilist need not be the only storyteller. Children are
often eager to share their knowledge of stories and the
stories of their lives. Frequently, the entire gathering of
children tell one story together. Once discovered, the
story of God's presence is simple and without ending, as
God's love is unending. It is a story that appeals to all ages
as it grows about us and within us.

Related to the storytelling and listening skills, the
homilist also develops *skills in meditating* with children on
their lives. With these skills, the homilist is able to ask
questions to which only the child has the answer, or
to which there may be no right or wrong answer. We
undermine the child's natural sense of wonder when we

ask only those questions to which the child knows we already have answers. On the other hand, contemplation nurtures in children their sense of wonder and provides them with access to the silence of the Spirit within them.

We adults often mistakenly presume the attention span of children is short. Observe how long even very young children can be absorbed by watching an ant or caterpillar. Consider how often children will listen with rapt attention to the same story, over and over again. Although children may reflect in what may seem to us distracted ways, they are natural contemplatives. Even in our manic-media world, children can be watching television while thinking intently about something else.

The skillful homilist walks with children in these ways, reassuring them with the story of the journey of Jesus and of all the people of God who have walked in the light of the Spirit. This means that the homilist reflects prayerfully not only on the scriptures but also on the word expressed—breathed out—in the lives of the children.

If the homilist is to facilitate the prayer of the children, then *the homilist must be a person who is both reflective and prayerful.* To be reflective is to listen with the heart to God's self-revelation both in the word and in the lives of the children. To be prayerful is to be watchful of and open to the movement of the Spirit, as it is the Spirit who moves us to pray.

Interpreting the Scriptures

When the homilist studies the scriptures in preparation for gathering with the assembly of both adults *and children*, a new sense of reality sets in. Children have a way of seeing with simplicity and clarity. After a reading from *Isaiah* one Sunday morning, a homilist began her reflections by asking the children, "What is a prophet?" The children replied with blank stares. As the homilist tried to answer her own question, the children grew restless; the power of the imagery of the lion sleeping with

the lamb was being drained from them. The experience of
a prophetic vision was being lost on the attempt to convey
an understanding of the word *prophet*.

As everyone knows, there is no end to the study of the
scriptures. Nor is there any limit to the amount of study
homilists should embrace both privately and with others.
Adults are quick to recognize a homilist performing a
needless biblical biopsy. Children are restless to tolerate
it. Whether serving assemblies of adults, children, or any
combination thereof, the prepared homilist is one who
knows what to leave out. We gather to eat the fruit, not
prune the vines.

Often the lay person who serves as a homilist for
children is called because the individual has the ability to
communicate with children. Frequently, the person has
experience as a classroom teacher or catechist and knows
how to involve children. Teaching background and the
attending methods of involving children, while valuable,
may get in the way when applied in a liturgical setting. We
will explore some of those differences later. The point we
want briefly to make here is this: Skill in communicating
with children in a liturgical setting requires of the homilist
a personal, biblical spirituality and knowledge of how to
draw children into the scriptures as participants in rather
than observers of the story of God's love. When God's
word is written in homilists' hearts we run less risk of
using methods of involving children that call attention to
themselves rather than to God's presence in the word.

If your parish does not supply homilists with biblical
resources, you may want to make such an investment your
contribution to the parish. We have included in this book
a bibliography of selected resources. Several Bible
commentaries are available. You will also find a good Bible
dictionary invaluable, one that gives background to passages
and words. You can also obtain commentaries that accom-
pany the children's lectionaries, both the one endorsed for
liturgical use by the Canadian bishops as well as the one

approved for experimental use by the U.S. bishops.[4]

Knowledge of the scriptures is especially needed when proclaiming the word to children in language they can understand. While the children's lectionary endorsed by the Canadian bishops addresses children as young as six years old, the U.S. bishops' lectionary seems to be intended for older children, aged 9 to 12 years.

The introduction to the U.S. bishops' lectionarys tates: "The hearers of the word for whom this work is primarily intended are children of elementary grades (preadolescents)" (Introduction, Part III, Section B, Paragraph 15).[5] While the expression "elementary grades" is sometimes taken to include primary grades (that is, grades 1, 2, and 3), the term "preadolescents" normally means children no younger than 9 and up to 12 years old. (The introduction also footnotes Paragraph 6 of the *Directory for Masses With Children* which states, "The directory is concerned with children who have not yet entered the period of pre-adolescence."[6]) Aside from this ambiguity over the intended audience, the introduction does state that the U.S. bishops' lectionary is "primarily" for older ("preadolescent") children. This focus primarily on older children presents a problem for homilists when using the U.S. bishops' lectionary.

A recent survey shows that children who attend the separate Liturgy of the Word fall into the following age groupings: Under 5 years old—10.58%; 5 to 6 years old—29.18%; 7 to 9 years old—40.78%; 10 to 12 years old—17.58%; over 12 years old—1.88%.[7] This means that the U.S. bishops' lectionary does not address the large majority of children—perhaps 70%—who attend separate liturgies of the word. What's a homilist to do?

While respectful of the authority of the U.S. bishops' conference, you will need to adapt the lectionary to accommodate the particular children in your assembly, or use the lectionary endorsed for liturgical use by the Canadian bishops. In either case, when faced with real children in a particular gathering, you may need to further adapt whatever lectionary you may be using.

As the *Directory for Masses With Children* affirms, our responsibility is to do what is to the "spiritual advantage" of the children (Paragraph 44).[8] Whatever children's lectionary we might use, we have the further responsibility to do our homework in the scriptures before proclaiming the word adapted for children. The importance of having children hear God speak in language they can understand further highlights the need for homilists to have and to use biblical resources and a variety of translations.

Clearly, it is vital that homilists be faithful to the word and to the history of the church's interpretation of the scriptures. "It is the faith of the church that the preacher must proclaim, not merely his (sic) own. . . . The qualified preacher will lead his (sic) people to ever greater unity of faith among themselves as well as with prior generations of believers."[9]

Interpreting the Lives of Children

The homilist is also required to be faithful to the children and in touch with their experience in society today. Children also suffer the consequences of the pressures parents endure in their efforts to provide physical, psychological, and emotional security for their children. Children now depend upon a variety of people to provide the nurturing that traditional families in tightly-knit communities formerly provided.

Homilists cannot, obviously, solve the problems of children in the assembly. We can, nevertheless, give them recognition, let them know that they count, that we value their presence among us. We can reassure them with our personal expressions of comfort and understanding. We can be sensitive to their fragile feelings of rejection and condemnation. In even the smallest gesture of kindness, we can be a sign to them of God's enduring compassion. We can encourage and give them strength to care for one another in a world that often shows little care. In other words, we can show them where care comes from and to be creators of a caring community.

The exposure of children to constant stimulation— from shopping malls to entertainment media—affect the way children both experience life and articulate their experiences. The qualified homilist is familiar with the images children use from the media to communicate their sense of what is real.

This is not to suggest that the homilist copy current manners of speech in order to let children know "you're one of them." Children want us to be ourselves. They look to us for wisdom and understanding. They want to know from us what they can trust of the world presented to them in electronic, digital wonder. They look to us for affirmation in their struggle to interpret life and find meaning in an on-again, off-again world, fickle and filled with enticing distractions.

It is a mistake to try to compete with media in order to entertain children into an appreciation of God's word. Such efforts only cheapen the Good News. The promise of slick commercials exploits without fulfilling the hunger of people for the Promise of life everlasting that only the reign of God brings. The qualified homilist's own person communicates the excitement of the God of unfailing love who is full of surprises . . . and more. Our God not only keeps promises but fulfills them beyond our most extravagant expectations.

Homilists Are Human

Rabbi Abraham Heschel once observed, "I am born a human being; what I have to acquire is being human."[10] That can be a humbling thought, particularly to any homilist who strives to take on the nature of the divine. We are not called to be divine. We are called to be human, as Christ Jesus was human. If, by so doing, we reflect what

some might call "the divine," that is not our reflection nor
our doing. It is God's reflection and God's doing.

Drawing from the wisdom and rich African-American
biblical spirituality of Charlie Robinson: When we gather
in the presence of our God, humility is the measure of
our humanity.

Charlie Robinson is one of God's surprises, with the
soul of a homilist. I met Mr. Robinson while working on a
documentary video in Mississippi with the late Sister Thea
Bowman. Mr. Robinson owns a GARAGE, with large
hand-painted lettering on its corrugated, galvanized metal
siding, that stands out like an icon in the sweltering
southern sun. A small OFFICE room of the same metal
siding, with its own entrance, stuck onto the side of the
larger building as an afterthought. I had often driven past
Mr. Robinson's GARAGE with more important things to do
(of course) than to stop.

Little seemed to be going on there. The truck-size
GARAGE door was always open but revealed only dark
shadows inside. The bright sun caught an auto engine
hanging heavy from a chain just inside the door to the left,
opposite the OFFICE. I saw only an occasional vehicle, in
obvious need of the MECHANIC, parked in the gravel
driveway.

Then, one day, I could no longer resist whatever was
slowing my late-model rental car as it neared this shrine.
I discovered Mr. Robinson in the OFFICE, seated in a
stuffed oil-stained chair with grease-coated arms and
surrounded by brown discarded boxes. He looked over the
top of his horn-rimmed glasses to greet me. In his muscular
mechanic's hands he held a tattered grease-soiled Bible.

I introduced myself, told him what I was doing in town,
and that I had stopped for no particular automotive reason,
just to visit, or maybe record some video of what folks do
and think about the things that mattered to them. Mr.
Robinson did not feel he had anything important to say
"for television." He was, nevertheless, willing to visit.

He told me he was retired from a factory job. He continued to work part-time at his garage "to keep busy," but his main interest was in "prison ministry."

"I go every week," he said. "We talk. Sometimes read the Bible."

"Do you have a favorite passage from the Bible?" I asked.

His face lit up. "There's lots," he said. "I'd have to think."

His thick fingers turned page after worn page with careful deliberation. Then he stopped, looked up over his eyeglasses again at me, and said, "I like all those about being 'umble."

"About being humble?" I repeated, to be sure I understood.

"Stand 'umble before the Lord," he said. "That's the part I like. That's how you tell about a man."

That's how you tell about a homilist, too.

If there is one quality that wraps up all of the attributes of a homilist for children (or adults), it is humility.

The word *humble* comes from a Latin word meaning *ground*. Homilists who are humble, like Charlie Robinson, are of the earth. Their hands know the very ground of life, the ground into which God breathed the breath of life.

Children are fresh from the ground, from the breath of God's life.

Homilists who walk humbly with children do not pretend to know more than the children or they themselves know. Humility is the product of knowledge of one's self, of one's ground. Such knowledge liberates us from having to pretend. Without pretensions, homilists are free to explore with children the ground of their being, confident in the knowledge that together they will discover there the breath of God's own Spirit.

With meekness of spirit, the homilist is able to take delight with children in God's surprises. God's word has a

way of enabling us to turn stones with the excitement of
children eager to see what lies hidden there. The search
for what eye cannot see engages the imagination whereby
we find access to the vision of the face of God.

Standing before the Lord and the assembly of children,
the homilist serves best when living in the childlike spirit
of the psalmist whom Jesus quoted in his Sermon on the
Mount:

"Blessed are the meek and humble of heart,
    for they shall inherit the kingdom of God"
    (*Psalm* 37:11; *Matthew* 5:5).

Summary

We have reflected here upon some of the qualities and
qualifications of the homilist, whether that person be an
ordained priest or a lay person who is particularly gifted
in communicating with children and who presides at
children's liturgies of the word. Both priest and lay person
share in the dignity of the priesthood which ultimately
rests in the people who are the body of Christ.

• The role of the homilist is to facilitate the public
prayer of those gathered.

• The homilist is a servant of God's word. As servant,
the homilist walks with children, listening with them and
to them with wonder and awe as they share with us their
original experiences of God's presence in their lives.

• The homilist requires a variety of skills, including
listening, storytelling, and *meditating*; each of these flows
from a prayerful and reflective person, nourished by a rich
biblical and liturgical spirituality in harmony with the life
and work of Christ.

• The task of the homilist is not to teach our children
the scriptures, nor even to interpret the scriptures for our
children; rather, one of the homilist's principle tasks is to
guide and enlighten our children's reflections on their

lives with the light of the scriptures and to respond with praise and good works.

• The homilist is human and humble, which comes from a Latin word meaning "ground." So are homilists of the earth, rooted in the ground into which God breathed the very breath of life.

REFLECTIONS

1. Describe what is for you several of the most important points, insights, or thoughts that you have drawn from this chapter. Why do you consider these matters of importance?

2. How would you describe the role of the homilist? In what sense is the homilist a "servant of the Word"?

3. Explore the ramifications of praising God with thanks: How do we do that in the Liturgy of the Word? How does the homilist facilitate this response to God's goodness?

4. Based on your experience as a homilist or on your experience of listening to homilists, give examples to illustrate *listening skills, storytelling skills, skills in meditation*. What other skills do you consider important for homilists to develop?

5. In what sense does the homilist "interpret the scriptures" in the ritual setting? How does the purpose of this "interpretation" differ from Bible study or the place of the scriptures in a catechetical setting?

6. In what sense does the homilist "interpret the lives of children"? In what sense do children "interpret" their lives? How does the homilist serve children in their interpretations of their lives in light of the scriptures?

7. How would you describe some of the basic qualities of the homilist as a person?

8. Explore the ways in which you, as a homilist, follow the basic principle of the *Directory for Masses With Children*: to do what is to the "spiritual advantage" of children. How does this principle influence your use of scripture texts? Your adaptation of texts? Your responsibility to be true to the message of the texts?

9. How does your experience as a homilist and of homilists complement or conflict with the homilist as portrayed in this chapter?

10. How would you complete the following statements?
a. Qualities I admire in a homilist are. . . .
b. My strengths as a homilist are. . . .
c. The areas in which I would like to grow as a homilist are. . . .
d. I plan to improve myself by. . . .

FOOTNOTES

[1] *Fulfilled in Your Hearing: The Homily in the Sunday Assembly*, The Bishops' Committee on Priestly Life and Ministry, NCCB, © 1982 United States Catholic Conference, Inc., Washington, D.C., p. 9.

[2] Gerard S. Sloyan, *Worshipful Preaching*, © 1984 by Fortress Press, Philadelphia, p. 16.

[3] *Ibid.*, p. 17.

[4] Commentaries on the children's lectionaries, the U.S. bishops' lectionary for children, and the Canadian bishops' lectionary are available through Treehaus Communications, Inc., P.O. 249, Loveland, OH 45140-0429.

[5] *Lectionary for Masses With Children/Sundays of Cycle B, Introduction*, 1993 by The Order of St. Benedict, Inc., Collegeville, Minnesota, p. xviii.

[6] *Directory for Masses With Children*, © 1973 United States Catholic Conference of Bishops, p. 2.

[7] *CIC UPDATE* Newsletter, Volume 4 Number 1, Spring 1993, and Volume 4 Number 4, Winter 1993-94, © 1993 by Treehaus Communications, Inc., Loveland, OH.

[8] *Directory for Masses With Children*, © 1973 United States Conference of Catholic Bishops, p. 13.

[9] *Fulfilled in Your Hearing: The Homily in the Sunday Assembly*, p. 13.

[10] Abraham Joshua Heschel, *The Insecurity of Freedom*, © 1966 by Abraham Joshua Heschel; Farrar, Straus & Giroux, New York, p. 26.

Chapter Six

THE HOMILY: A RITUAL ACT

Then little children were brought to Jesus for him to place his hands on them and pray for them.

Matthew 19:13

The homily is a particular form of communication. It is part of liturgical, ritual activity. This distinguishes it from catechetics, a lecture, a sermon, or Bible study. As part of a ritual act, the homily at its best does not call attention to the homilist or interfere with the movement of the ritual. The homily's purpose is to facilitate the assembly's ritualized celebration of their faith in Jesus Christ. Therefore, "the homily presupposes faith"[1] in the community's members and speaks to them in the language of faith.

"One of the most important, and most specifically human, ways in which faith is communicated to individuals and communities is through language. The way we speak about our world expresses the way we think about it and interpret it. One of the reasons we speak about our world at all is to share our vision of the world with others. The preacher is a Christian specially charged with sharing the Christian vision of the world as the creation of a loving

God. Into this world human beings unleashed the powers
of sin and death. These powers have been met, however,
by God through his (sic) Son, Jesus Christ, in whom he
(sic) is at work not only to restore creation, but to
transform it into a new heaven and a new earth."[2]

Baptized into Christ's life and work, children share
fully in the faith of the assembly. But what is the faith of
children and how does the homily communicate in faith
with children?

Communicating in Faith With Children

Developmental theorists have made various efforts to
describe the evolving faith of children and the child's
capacity for religious experience.[3] Our purpose here is
not to explore those contributions, as helpful as they can
be. Their use in homiletics can needlessly complicate
efforts to make the homily a ritual rather than rational
action. This is not to say homilies are mindless or irrational.

At its best, the homily is an experience of symbol
(word) that communicates God's presence across
developmental stages, not to mention across individual
levels of mental, emotional, and psychological limitations.
The mystery of God's overflowing love surrounds each
person, regardless of one's human condition or our
individual capacities to realize God's love or respond to it.

In other words, as obvious as it may seem, God does not
love a child progressively more as the child develops new
skills, understandings, and maturity. We may use the
work of developmentalists to better understand the
evolving capacities of children. Stages of development
serve us not as categories into which children are rigidly
placed but as guidelines to help us know what children
need for further growth and development.

Children do not grow up in zip-lock bags from one stage
to another. As we have observed in previous chapters,
children grow up surrounded by an incredibly complex set
of influences, the product of human—though not always

humane—creativity. We do the best we can to respond
with sensitivity to the fragile mystery of life that pulses
within each child. We want to help our children
distinguish in our society those influences that
dehumanize us from those that nourish the human
spirit. We try to do this by affirming in our children a
vision of the reign of God.

The homily is a reflection on our lives in light of the
story of God's love and, necessarily, involves the use of
reason. We use our intelligence and our ability to reason,
however, in service of our experience of God's gift of faith.
This is why, as we explored in chapter four, it is important
that we proclaim the word in language children can
understand. As a ritual though nonetheless intelligible
action, the homily articulates the vision of the reign of
God and thereby influences the attitude with which
children view their lives.

Nurturing the Attitude of Faith

Attitude is another word for faith. Perhaps it is more
precise to say that attitude is a *reflection* of one's faith
which, as a gift from God, is more than one's attitude.
Like faith, attitude describes the way we view life and
stand in relationship with ourselves, others, our world, and
God. The story or myth that people of faith share with
children conveys to them a particular view of life which is
a product of God's gift of faith. Our Christian view of life—
our myth—influences the attitude with which children
view and, with God's grace, live their lives.

As used here, myth is not intended to mean a story that
is not so. On the contrary, myth is the story people tell in
order to reveal the most profound truth of their lives and
to describe a vision that makes life worth living.

Our faith—view of life or attitude—enables us to see
what appears not, to stand in the light of truth and survive
in spite of the surrounding darkness. What a saving gift
this is to us all, particularly, for example, to those children

so abused that they cannot distinguish themselves from
the darkness they experience, a darkness that many do not
pierce until, as adults, they look back to face the reality
that the darkness hid from their view.

Myth & Ritual: Media of Mystery

Story (myth) and ritual—in contrast to scientific
inquiry—are primary and primitive media of mystery.
Drawing from a story outside the Christian tradition—
though nonetheless insightful—consider the nursery
rhyme story *Humpty Dumpty*:
"Humpty Dumpty sat on the wall.
Humpty Dumpty had a great fall.
All the king's horses and all the king's men
couldn't put Humpty together again."
Enough said.
We are left now to wonder: Who was Humpty Dumpty?
Is that name male or female? How and why did (s)he fall?
Did (s)he slip? Was (s)he pushed? How did (s)he get up
onto the wall to begin with? What wall was (s)he sitting
on? Why couldn't the king's men and horses do anything
about this tragedy? Why did they want to put Humpty
together again? Were they afraid the king might have
thought they caused Humpty to fall? We are hard-pressed
for answers, simple as the story may be.
The story invites us to look beyond its details, to reach
into our own experiences of brokenness or, if we identify
with the king or his men, our own inability to repair our
own broken lives or those of people we may meet.
What does this story tell us about our own lives? Have
we ever felt fallen and broken? Has anything like this ever
happened to us, something that no earthly power could fix?
And the questions go on and on . . . .
Like this reflection on the nursery rhyme version of
The Fall, the homily cuts across age differences by telling
no more than is needed to draw the assembly into a
suspended state of wonder. Each person—whether 6 or 60

years old—brings to the story a lifetime to explore in light
of Humpty Dumpty's fall.

On the other hand, to follow the story with an analysis
of the egg, its fragile structure, and the impossibility of
reconstructing a shattered egg would quickly kill whatever
fresh vision of life the story might bring. Such an analysis
may eventually help to develop an appreciation for the
imagery of the story. However, the homily is not the place
for that, particularly with children, who walk in the garden
of faith still naked.

Although God fully graces children with faith, they
have yet to *hear the story*.

Those are loaded words. Some adults, too, have yet to
hear the story. Often we think we get the message and are
ready to move on to less boring and more serious matters
once we know that Humpty Dumpty is an egg. Or is this
image merely a story illustrator's assumption? How does
the egg enhance the story's truth? Matters not? Beware.
We face assemblies wherein rest those whom G.K.
Chesterton described as "dull" Christians: those of us who
are bored to death by the constant repetition of a story we
have never heard.

Responding in Praise and in Deed

The story homilists have to tell gives life and meaning
to our ritual. The homily is the point at which myth and
ritual intersect and become interwoven with our lives.
This moment, when at its best, moves those who *hear the
story* to breath out a sound that surely is of the Spirit:
"Aha!" When we hear the story as God's own self-
revelation *in our lives*, then our ritual-making response
takes on meaning that is also of God's making. Our ritual
response is the beginning of our share in making the
myth—the reign of God—a reality. The delicate task of the
homilist is to unfold for children this vision of the world
and attitude toward life so that they might make the reign

of God—which they already possess—a reality for us all.

This task requires respect for children, sensitivity to their imaginations and to the innate power of the story, as the simple Humpty Dumpty rhyme illustrates. The homily, at its best, taps into those universal concrete images through which God speaks to us with such simplicity and love that we will want to live in God's image of generous love. So will those hear who have ears to hear, regardless of age, state, or stage of life.

Chances are, the homily that speaks in the concrete ritual language of faith will reach both children and adults. The homily that reduces the ritual language of faith to rational discourse will reach neither children nor adults, and risks visiting upon the assembly a gospel that is more burdensome than liberating. Rational discourse defines rather than describes, draws conclusions without drawing pictures, makes sense without appealing to the senses, fills the mind without engaging the imagination.

Too often, homilists feel compelled to use the scriptures to admonish members of the assembly for their behavior. This is not to ignore those scripture texts which do chastise people for their uncaring conduct. However, such moral exhortations are to be situated in the context of God's loving embrace, not rejection.

Children are sensitive to our admonitions, particularly when they hear them proclaimed by us with the ritual authority of the "pulpit." We risk having them leave with the message that to follow Jesus requires conforming to a code of conduct or set of rules. Those who keep the rules are worthy of God's love; those who don't fall out of favor with God. The experience can produce in children behavior motivated not by gratitude for God's generous love, but by fear and guilt. Consider the ramifications for our children today.

More children than we realize come to us already with low self-esteem, often the result of emotional or physical abuse. These children already believe they are bad and

despair of ever winning God's favor. The image of a
rejecting rather than loving God verifies for them their
sense of despair and reinforces their lack of self-worth.
Children, on the other hand, whose self-esteem is healthy,
are no better served by the image of a God whose favor
needs to be won. We only risk confusing these children,
causing them to wonder: "What kind of God is this who
does not feel good about me when I feel so good about
myself?" They intuitively know that such an image of God
is incompatible with their sense of self-worth.

Children with high self-esteem can fail and still feel
good about themselves. They can learn from failure.
Moreover, when they may fail in their relationship with
God, the experience can deepen their sense of God's love
for them, rather than alienate them from God. Their
confidence both in themselves and in God motivates them
to move beyond any guilt they may have felt and to start
anew, to try again, unburdened by any need to win approval.

David Heller reports on his interviews with Jewish,
Catholic, Baptist, and Hindu children: ". . . A concern with
guilt and purity is most endemic in the group of Catholic
children. . . . Eleven-year-old Laura displays her guilt
concerning the existential human condition of poverty. In
her 'child alone' scenario, her deity descends to the little
girl's play room and firmly states, 'Next time you have
your birthday you are to give the children of the poor a
toy or doll.' . . . Sometimes, the children seem to believe
the guilt is deserved and that the deity is legitimately
bestowing that guilt. At other times, the children seem to
question their guilt and thus frequently undergo a difficult
cycle of guilt and anger toward the deity."[4]

The homily can serve to nurture healthy attitudes in
children rather than visit on children the kind of guilt
Heller describes. The homily can celebrate with children
the presence of a God who frees us all from guilt with
unfailingly forgiving love, a God who reigns with
compassion and mercy. When our children realize God's

generosity, God's good grace will move them to respond both in prayerful gratitude and with the desire to share God's generous love with one another. In other words, our children can come to realize their sense of self-worth is well founded. They can take pleasure in knowing that they are, as Paul so eloquently put it, temples of God, dwelling places of the Spirit. In a word: "holy" (*1 Corinthians* 3:16, 17).

The Lectionary and the Homily

When we reflect with children on the vision of the reign of God, we nourish our reflections with readings from the scriptures. The biblical image of the "reign of God" is intended here to mean those events, places, and times when people show one another the kind of compassion, care, and forgiveness that is of God. In such ways does God's self-revelation—God's Word becoming flesh—continue to happen in human history. This is the on-going self-revelation of God we ritualize in our liturgical celebrations.

The lectionary provides the homilist with a selection of readings that complement the feasts and seasons of the Liturgical Year. These readings carry the assembly through a comprehensive meditation on the story of God's self-revelation, focusing particularly on the life and work of God's own Son, our Lord, Jesus.

Lectionaries for children have been prepared in order to enable children to hear the story of God's love proclaimed at liturgical gatherings in language they can understand. Based upon the principles outlined by the *Directory for Masses With Children*, the introduction to the U.S. bishops' lectionary for children states, "In adapting the liturgy for use with children, the Church's goal is to nourish their faith and lead them to 'active, conscious, and authentic' participation in the worship of the whole assembly, but not to establish a different rite for children" (Paragraph 11).[5]

In an effort to serve the particular needs of children in local assemblies, the U.S. bishops recommend even further adaptations. For example, "liturgical planners, with the consent of the priest celebrant, may further adapt particularly long readings by choosing to use only that part of the selection which presents a particular biblical image or is directly related to the other reading(s)" (Paragraph 18).[6]

The reason for such adaptations is to accommodate both the children and the character of the Liturgy of the Word as a ritual prayer. "The Liturgy of the Word is neither a catechetical session nor an introduction to biblical history. The liturgy celebrates the word of God in narrative and song, makes it visible in gesture and symbol and culminates in the celebration of the eucharist" (Paragraph 24).[7]

The U.S. bishops make the same point in their guidelines for homilists. "The goal of the liturgical preacher is not to interpret a text of the Bible (as would be the case in teaching a Scripture class) as much as to draw on the texts of the Bible as they are presented in the lectionary to interpret peoples' lives . . . in such a way that they will be able to celebrate Eucharist. . . ."[8]

Some of the readings in the lectionary, however, are particularly problematic for children. Even when using a lectionary expressly for children, you may face a particular group of children for whom the reading is inappropriate or inadequately adapted. For example, in the children's lectionary approved for experimental use by the U.S. bishops' conference, the gospel for the 6th Sunday of Easter/Year B begins in this way: "Jesus said to his disciples: 'I have loved you, just as my Father has loved me. So make sure that I keep on loving you. If you obey me, I will keep loving you, just as my Father keeps loving me, because I have obeyed him. I have told you this to make you as completely happy as I am. . . .' " (*John* 15:9-12).

This translation risks communicating an image of God

whose love is propositional or conditional. The message of the passage, as rendered, will be clear to children and, in its clarity, risks clearly misleading them. The same passage taken from the adult lectionary reads this way: "Jesus said to his disciples: 'As the Father has loved me, so I have loved you. Live on in my love. You will live in my love if you keep my commandments, even as I have kept my Father's commandments, and live in his love. All this I tell you that my joy may be yours and your joy may be complete' " (*John* 15:9-12).

The implication of the text is not that God will stop loving those who fail to keep God's commandments. Nor is the message about how to *win* God's love. The message is one of *guidance in how to live in* God's love, how to find *joy* in loving others as God loves us: by following God's commandments as Jesus did. Not to "live in God's love" is *our* choice, not God's. Though we may fail, God's love is unfailing. God is always ready to forgive, just as Jesus forgave even unto death on the cross.

The *Directory for Masses With Children* recommends a solution to such problems. The selection or adaptation of any text is to be guided primarily by the "spiritual advantage which the readings can offer children" (Paragraph 44). It would be of greater spiritual advantage to the children if such a passage were rendered this way: "Jesus said to his disciples, 'I love you just as God loves me. Live always in my love. If you keep my commandments, you are living in my love. I am telling you this so that you may be completely filled with my joy' " (*John* 15:9-11).[9] Surely this is joy-filling Good News of God's love in which homilists will want to rejoice with children.

Summary

We have drawn heavily in this chapter on the guidelines described in the handbook *Fulfilled In Your Hearing* compiled by the Bishops' Committee on Priestly

Life and Ministry. Although the bishops' handbook does
not focus explicitly on children in the assembly, we have
attempted to follow those guidelines while keeping in
mind an even more fundamental principle drawn from the
Directory for Masses With Children—that is: Just as our
selection and adaptation of readings must be guided by
whatever serves the spiritual advantage of our children, so,
too, must our homilies be so guided.

We will continue to apply this principle as we explore in
the following chapter the form and style of the homily. So,
too, will we be building upon the characteristics of the
homily that we developed briefly in this chapter:

● The homily for children—as for adults—is part of our
ritual activity and distinct from catechetics, a lecture, or
Bible study.

● The purpose of the homily is to facilitate our
children's ritualized celebration of their faith in Jesus
Christ, whose life and work we celebrate in the feasts and
seasons of the Liturgical Year.

● The homily guides the children's reflection on their
lives in light of the story of God's love.

● The story or myth that people of faith share with
children conveys to our children a particular view of life
which is a product of God's gift of faith and of God's own
initiative.

● The story homilists have to tell gives life and
meaning to our ritual.

● The vision with which each homily looks at life comes
from the lectionary, a selection of scripture readings that
throughout the year carry our children through a
comprehensive meditation on the story of God's
self-revelation in Jesus Christ.

● Our use of the lectionary with children, including
lectionaries adapted for children, is guided by one

over-riding principle: we must do what is to the spiritual advantage of our children.

REFLECTIONS

1. In what sense is the homily a ritual act? How does it differ from Bible study and catechetics?

2. How does the homily nurture faith? In what sense is myth the medium by which we communicate our faith? What is the relationship between myth and ritual as media of faith?

3. What is it about the concrete, biblical language of metaphor that conveys a sense of the mystery of God's presence?

4. Give some examples of the ritual language of faith. How does this language differ from that of systematic theology or doctrinal formulations?

5. How does the experience of children affect their hearing of God's word? What are some of the cautions homilists need to take in communicating with children in our society, such as, for example, with those children who have been abused or with those who have been over-indulged with things?

6. How would you describe the relationship of the lectionary to the homily? Why is it important at times to further adapt even those lectionaries especially prepared for children?

7. Examine the way in which your homilies reflect—or fail to reflect—the use of concrete biblical language and images; what do you need to do to improve your use of the ritual language of symbol that appeals to our children's imaginations?

FOOTNOTES

[1] *Fulfilled in Your Hearing: The Homily in the Sunday Assembly*, The Bishops' Committee on Priestly Life and Ministry, NCCB, © 1982 United States Catholic Conference, Inc., Washington, D.C., p. 17.

[2] *Ibid.*, pp. 18-19.

[3] W. Alan Smith, *Children Belong In Worship*, © 1984 by CBP Press, St. Louis, Missouri. See chapter two on the psychology of human development.

[4] David Heller, *The Children's God*, © 1986 University of Chicago Press, Chicago, pp. 27-28.

[5] *The Lectionary for Masses With Children/Sundays of Cycle B, Introduction.* Approved for experimental use by the U.S. Conference of Catholic Bishops, © 1993 by The Order of St. Benedict, Inc., Collegeville, Minnesota, p. xv.

[6] *Ibid.*, p. xvii.

[7] *Ibid.*, p. xviii.

[8] *Fulfilled in Your Hearing: The Homily in the Sunday Assembly*, p. 20.

[9] *The SUNDAY Book of Readings: A Lectionary for Children* (Year B). Endorsed for liturgical use by the Canadian Conference of Catholic Bishops, © 1992 by Forum Katecheticum. Treehaus Communications, Inc. Loveland, OH, p. 51.

Part Three

THE PRACTICE OF
HOMILETICS
FOR CHILDREN

Chapter Seven

THE HOMILY:
STYLE & STRUCTURE

Jesus said, "Let the little children come to me, and do not hinder them, for the kingdom of heaven belongs to such as these."

Matthew 19:14

The God in whose presence we gather has come *personally* to love us and to live with us in Christ Jesus. It is fitting that our style of communicating with children be as personal as was Jesus' style. We may have disciples in the assembly who want to keep children away, as did the disciples in the time of Jesus. Or, we may have homilists who simply ignore our children who assemble with us. Jesus neither refused nor ignored children. On the contrary, he became indignant with those who tried to keep children "in their place." Jesus said, "Let the children come to me" (*Mark* 10:14).

The word *homily* comes from a Greek word *homileo*, the use of which "in the New Testament implies a more personal and conversational form of address than that used by the classical Greek orator. . . . A homily should sound more like a personal conversation, albeit a conversation on matters of utmost importance, than like a speech or a classroom lecture. What we should strive for is a style that is purposeful and personal, avoiding whatever sounds casual and chatty on the one extreme or impersonal and detached on the other."[1]

Children are particularly sensitive to the *manner* or *style* in which we speak with them, even more than to the words we use. Recall the lady who remembered from her childhood the warmth and kindness of the preacher and the way in which he told Bible stories. Our manner or style is an integral part of both our communication and the message. It reveals our attitude toward both the children and God's word. Recall our earlier observation in chapter 6: *attitude* is a *reflection* of our faith. Our style reveals whether or not we ourselves see the assembly as an expression of Christ's presence.

The recognition of Christ's presence in the assembly affects the way in which we reflect with the assembly on God's word. Our style reveals that awareness when we use the homily not as a means of instruction or exhortation but as a meditation on the assembly's life of faith. In other words, we explore the ramifications of God's word as it comes to bear on our lives. While this meditation may incidentally be instructive and, depending upon the particular scripture text, it may sometimes be an exhortation, the primary focus of the homily is the reign of God as it bears upon our lives here and now.

In our homily with children, we explore God's word in a manner that opens the way for the children themselves to discover the relationship between, on the one hand, God's self-revelation throughout human history as it comes to us in the scriptures and, on the other hand, God's self-revelation here and now as it emerges through our children's original experiences of God's presence in their lives. By so doing, the homily continually deepens the awareness of our children to the mystery of God's unfailing love. This interplay between our children's original experiences of God and the word of God proclaimed enables our children to feel that they belong to God's family, that their lives are precious to God.

Style in Relation to Structure

Style is directly related to the form or structure of the homily. In the remaining part of this chapter, we will explore the classical form of inquiry as a homily structure or homiletic process for use with children—or, for that matter, with adults. It includes three inter-related steps: observe, judge, and act. In the context of homiletics, to observe is to *listen* to God speak to us; to judge is to *reflect* upon the reign of God in relation to my life; to act is to *respond* with gratitude expressed in praise and in the practice of good works, making God's reign a reality in our lives today.

This inquiry structure or process particularly respects the homily as "a scriptural interpretation of human existence which enables a community to recognize God's active presence, to respond to that presence in faith through liturgical word and gesture, and beyond the liturgical assembly, through a life lived in conformity with the Gospel."[2]

Let us explore now how the process might broadly unfold. In chapter nine we will follow the process with sample scripture texts.

I. *We listen to God speak.*

We can express the focus of this first step in terms of these two generic questions:

1. *How might I awaken in our children, gathered here with me, a sense of God's presence here and now?*

2. *What might our children, gathered here with me today, hear God saying to them in these particular readings?*

There are no formula answers to these closely related questions. We can get a clue to the second question, about

what the children might hear God saying to them, by
talking with some of the children as part of our
preparation. Such an exploration helps us to look at life
through the eyes of a child and prepare for how our
children might respond or what they might express during
the liturgy itself. In addition, however, we might also start
our homily by asking our children, "What did you hear?"

We can ask this question whether gathered with just a
few or several hundred children. Although each child may
have neither a chance nor the desire to answer openly, this
question invites our children to consider what they
individually hear God is saying, rather than simply upon
what they think we want them to hear. So, too, are we
acknowledging God's presence in the word and listening
ourselves to what God is saying to us.

Often children respond to the question, "What did you
hear?" by repeating what they heard. This will reveal how
well our children simply remember the reading. Of course,
without such knowledge our children cannot proceed with
any reflection on life in light of the word.

If our children are confused or don't have the facts of a
story clear, we return to the text and read it again. By so
doing, we call attention to God's word. We avoid the
temptation to interpret the reading for the children when
we are imparting God's word to them for their reflection
and interpretation.

In other words, we are careful not to tell the children
what we think they should hear. Rather, we ask the kind
of questions that draw attention away from us and onto
God's presence in the word and in the world. Moreover,
we affirm the children's answers, even though they may
seem farfetched to us. Such affirmation may come in the
form of another question, "Would you say more about
that?" Or, "How do you feel when you hear that?"

After hearing the story of the birth of Jesus, one
6-year-old child responded during the reflection on the
question, "What did you hear?" by saying, "I have a new

baby brother." The child connected with the story at the level of feeling. She felt the joy of the birth of Jesus as she did the joy of her baby brother's birth, even though she was not making all of the connections between the scripture text and her experience. A homilist with less sensitivity would perhaps have told the child that we can talk about her little brother later, but now we are taking about the birth of Jesus.

We can help our children hear God speaking to them by engaging their imaginations in the text itself. Drawing again on the Christmas narrative, one homilist invited the children to imagine they were shepherds attending their flocks on the night Jesus was born. Imagine going to the place of Jesus' birth. How would you describe what you see there? How would you be able to tell that this baby was Jesus, the Son of God? How would you feel about being there? What would you say to Mary? To Joseph? To Jesus?

Questions phrased in this way draw our children into the story as participants, rather than as spectators. Also, such questions cause our children to recall the details of the story without making their retelling of the story a kind of quiz to see whether they were listening.

Sometimes a homilist will follow the reading with a story or a description of a human situation that attempts to situate the message of the scripture text in a contemporary setting. Following this exploration, the homilist returns to the scripture text, interpreting the situation in light of the scriptures, thereby illustrating God's active presence in our lives today. The conclusion focuses on our response of praise and willingness to follow God's way.

While this practice may be appropriate at times, it also risks dismissing the original text as less valuable than our own selected situation or story. For children, the innate value of biblical imagery is its appeal to the imagination. Such appeal leads to the child's own discovery of the relationship between what the text reveals of God's

presence and the child's original experience of God's
presence in life today.

Too often we forget: children already bring to the
scripture texts their own personal and original experiences
of God's presence. We serve our children best by
restraining our desire to make those "connections" for
them. Moreover, by inviting our children into the
scripture text with its rich biblical imagery, we show
greater respect for their intelligence and we engage their
imaginations, supporting them in their search for the light
that their personal experiences shed on the scriptures and,
thereby, discovering the light that the scriptures shed on
their lives.

II. *We reflect on the reign of God.*

In this second step, we focus on two generic questions
that flow naturally from the earlier questions that dealt
with listening to God speak and helping our children to
hear what God has to say. The two additional questions are:

1. *How can I engage the children's imaginations in
what God is saying?*

2. *How can I guide the children to discover for themselves the relationship between God's word and their lives?*

Recall that we already began in the first step to engage
our children's imaginations by inviting them, for example,
to imagine they are the shepherds to whom the angel
announced the Good News of the Savior's birth.

We can further engage the imaginations of our children
by inviting them to imagine they are Mary and Joseph
trying to find a place to stay. How would you feel? What
would you do? Why do you suppose Jesus was born in a
borrowed stable among animals rather than in a
comfortable home? Why do you think ordinary shepherds
were the first to be told about the birth of Jesus? The
shepherds were attending their flocks in darkness; then
they saw a great light that first frightened them and then
filled them with joy. How do you feel when you are in

darkness, or when you are feeling the darkness of a sad heart? How would you describe the kind of light that would bring you joy? How might that light also seem scary? What does this story tell us about God's love for us?

Although our children may not grasp the historical context of biblical events, they can identify with the human experience that these events embrace. Such images as light and darkness, and such emotions as joy and fear, are not limited by time or place, culture or context, childhood or adulthood. Such biblical imagery is the very matter that feeds the imagination and provides access to the mystery of God's personal presence—which is both within and beyond time and place.

The object is to invite our children into this mystery by exploring with them questions to which we do not already have the answers. Gathering with a small number of children makes such a meditation all the more interactive, so that the content of our homily is drawn from the children's own reflections.

On the other hand, when we are gathered with a large assembly of children, we can still invite them to consider these questions although the size of the assembly may intimidate our children and we may not get a verbal response from many or any of them. With a larger gathering, we share our own imaginings and express a variety of responses based on our knowledge of our children who have gathered with us. Of course, this requires more communication with our children before we gather with them in the liturgical setting.

We continue to draw upon our children's imagination as we invite them to discover the relationship between God's word and their lives. Our inquiry might flow along these lines: Jesus was born a long, long time ago. Why do we still tell this story today and celebrate the coming of Jesus into our lives? Why did Jesus come to live with us? How would you describe the joy that the birth of Jesus brings into our lives today? In what way is Jesus the light of our

world today?   How would you describe the peace that
Jesus brings?

Such reflections lead us to the third and last step.

III. *We respond to God's word.*

The generic questions to consider in this final stage
include these two:

1. *How might I guide our children to make God's reign
a reality in their lives?*

2. *For what reason do we praise God and give thanks
today?*

As we enter this part of the homiletic process, we are
careful to inspire our children to respond with joy and
gratitude rather than to moralize or to burden our
children with admonitions to behave in a certain way or,
even worse, to feel guilty about their ways of life. For
instance, if we use the gifts children receive at Christmas
as evidence to demonstrate the poverty surrounding the
birth of Jesus, we risk making our children feel guilty
about whatever gifts they receive and, naturally, enjoy—
while Jesus had not even a place to lay his head.

Following again the Christmas readings, our line of
reflection aimed at letting God reign in our lives might
flow along these lines: What does the joyful response of
the shepherds tell us about the way we might respond to
the news of Jesus' birth today? How can we make it
possible for Jesus to be born in our lives today? How can
we share with others the presence of Jesus here and now?
How can we share with others the joy of Jesus with us?
How can we bring the peace of Jesus into our world today?
How can we follow the light of Jesus today? How can we be
a light for others?

As with the other two stages in this process, our object
is not to make applications for our children. Rather, we
seek to cooperate with the movement of the Spirit within
our children. We trust in the creative power of God's word,
in the belief that when God speaks, God creates. So do we

invite our children to express their praise and gratitude for what God has done for them, to let the Spirit create in them a new heart and, through their good works, to renew the face of the earth.

Summary

This suggested three-phase inquiry method, properly understood, complements the natural way we function as creatures endowed with human consciousness, imagination and intelligence. To be able to observe, judge, and act are powers that enable us to process and act upon our perceptions of human experience.

Actually, these three powers are operating all at once. In other words, when we are observing, we are also judging and acting upon our perceptions. Similarly, in the homiletic context, when we are "listening to God speak," we are also "reflecting" and "responding" on some level; that is, our listening is itself an action, and our reflecting is itself a response.

While we have separated these powers as stages in a homiletic process, their organic relationship to one another and to the way we humans function complements God's organic presence in human experience and, ultimately, human consciousness. Moreover, this process avoids creating an artificial structure that risks making the experience of God's presence artificial or a manipulation of our children's consciousness.

When we ritualize God's presence in the word with our children, we are celebrating a mystery beyond human comprehension. It is only fitting that we walk into that mystery with our children as we are, without contrivances, hidden agendas, preconceptions, or fixed expectations. As God's children, we, too, walk with hope and trust, arriving empty-handed before our God who, as the Negro spiritual expresses so well, has "the whole world in his hands . . . every tiny baby in his hands. . . ."

REFLECTIONS

1. What are for you the highlights of this chapter?

2. How does the style proposed in this chapter reflect the way Jesus communicated the gospel? In what sense does the homilist's style reveal the homilist's attitude toward both the assembly and God's word?

3. Why do you think it is important for the homily to be designed to invite the children to discover for themselves the relationship between their original experiences of God's presence and the story of God's saving presence throughout history? How might the homilist's style or the homily's structure get in the way of children finding harmony between their original experiences of God's presence and their hearing of God's word?

4. Describe in your own words and discuss the basic characteristics of each of these three steps or structural components:

> I.   We listen to God speak.
> II. We reflect on the reign of God.
> III. We respond to God's word.

5. In what way is the inquiry method—*observe, judge, act*—natural to the way people function as intelligent creatures? How does this process or method complement the function and purpose of the homily?

6. Discuss your answers and the ramifications of your answers to the questions proposed in each of three structural components:

> I.   *We listen to God speak.*
>> 1. How might I awaken in our children, gathered here with me, a sense of God's presence here and now?
>> 2. What might our children, gathered here with me today, hear God saying to them in these particular readings?

II. *We reflect on the reign of God.*
  1. How can I engage the children's imaginations
     in what God is saying?
  2. How can I guide the children to discover for
     themselves the relationship between God's
     word and their lives?
III. *We respond to God's word.*
  1. How might I guide our children to make God's
     reign a reality in their lives?
  2. For what reason do we praise God and give
     thanks today?

FOOTNOTES

[1] *Fulfilled in Your Hearing: The Homily in the Sunday
   Assembly*, NCCB, The Bishops' Committee on Priestly
   Life and Ministry, © 1982 United States Catholic
   Conference, Inc., Washington, D.C., p. 24.

[2] *Ibid.*, p. 29.

Chapter Eight

PREPARATION:
A GROUP PROCESS

Be imitators of God, therefore, as dearly loved children, and live in love, as Christ loved us . . .

Ephesians 5:1

An African proverb observes: "It takes a whole village to raise a child."

Certainly we can apply this proverb to raising—that is, initiating—children in the Christian community. When the parish community gathers, everyone there influences the raising of the community's children. Each of us who has any degree of contact with a child—parents, grandparents, brothers and sisters, friends, television producers, teachers, parish ministers, street car and school bus operators, neighbors, coaches, department and grocery store clerks—each plays a part in raising that child.

Homilists are significant members of the village that raises our children. We are the village storytellers. We guide the children's reflections on what lies hidden in their experience—God's active presence. So, when we prepare to tell that unending, unfolding story—God's story—we need the help of all the villagers to tell us about their experience of God's presence in their lives.

Preparing with a group complements what a homily is about: "A scriptural interpretation of human existence which enables a community to recognize God's active presence, to respond to that presence in faith through liturgical word and gesture, and beyond the liturgical assembly, through a life lived in conformity with the Gospel."[1]

The Homily Preparation Group

We are better able to speak with our children about what is important to them when we involve them in our preparation. One way to do this is by forming a small group of about four or five children with one or two parents to reflect with us on the readings. The ages of the children might vary from 8 or 9 to 12 years. We can keep the group fresh by rotating two or more members every 4 or 5 weeks.

If we have several lay homilists, we might form several such groups, with two homilists participating in each group. Again, we will want the group to include several children, with the group dynamic giving precedence to the children's reflections.

Another way to form a preparation group is by gathering weekly with all of the adults who serve as homilists off and on through the year. Let's say we have a team of 10 or 12 adult homilists. Presumably they are in touch with children and can represent the experience of children in their reflections on the scriptures. This preparation group of adults might involve all of these adults all of the time, or members might rotate in order to maintain a regular attendance of 5 or 6 members.

Whatever form our group may take, we will want to meet for no more than an hour on the Sunday or Monday before the Sunday when the Liturgy of the Word in preparation occurs. The homilist for the liturgy in preparation comes prepared to preside at this group meeting.

Personal Preparation

Our personal preparation might involve the same
steps we later will follow during the group meeting itself.
These include:

1. *We listen* to what God is saying. We read the texts
within the context of the scriptures. In other words, if a
reading comes from *Mark* 13:33-37, we read the entire
chapter 13. Listen to what God is saying *to me*, not
what we think God may be saying in the readings to
our children.

2. *We reflect* upon the texts and upon life today in light
of what God is saying to us individually *about my life*. At
this point, we delay interpreting the texts as they might
relate to our children's lives. We let God's word first
become part of our own individual lives. (Later, with the
preparation group we explore how the texts might relate to
the children's lives.)

3. *We respond* to God's word. Pray. Resolve to act
upon God's word—if even in the smallest way—in the spirit
of praise and gratitude.

These first three steps are intended to let God's word
take flesh in our own hearts, shape our attitudes, sharpen
our vision of the reign of God. Then, when we speak, we
do so out of our own personal faith.

4. *We research* the texts. After praying with the
scriptures, we might explore some of the commentaries—
but with caution. Particularly when preparing for a homily
with children, we want to be accurate in our interpretation
of the texts but not academic. Our challenge is to
unclutter ourselves so that we might hear, see, and speak
clearly with the simplicity of a child. We draw upon the
commentaries to achieve authentic simplicity and to avoid
becoming simplistic.

Sometimes we can best achieve simplicity by letting go
of what we consider so important to say. Let the word of

God have its say. Just as in conversations with one another, when we are too intent on what we want to say, we do not hear well what someone else is saying.

Following this personal preparation and meditation, we are ready to gather with the homily preparation group. In this gathering we meet another opportunity to hear God speak to us from within the experience of the community. The group's reflection might follow the same process.

Meeting With the Preparation Group

I. *We listen.*

1. *We listen to God's word* (5 minutes). First slowly read the gospel aloud, as it is this text that will usually receive our primary focus. Pause for enough time to allow participants to write down key words, phrases, images that strike them. Then slowly read one of the other two readings, response and gospel acclamation. We may also want to read both the Old Testament and New Testament readings, although usually more than one of these readings (and the gospel) is too much for children to deal with in a single liturgy. Pause again, as before, for participants to make brief notes.

2. *We listen to one another* (5 minutes). During this time, we each share what came to mind and heart while listening to the readings. We do not discuss or explore these impressions; we listen and reflect. This exchange helps the homilist discover what parts of the readings strike a particular chord with the participants. These responses can provide an insight into the lives of the assembly.

(Note: If the preparation group does not include children, the adult participants will want first to share their own personal reflections, for their own spiritual growth. Then they will want to share their thoughts on how the readings might strike the children they know.

What might our children hear God say to them in these readings?)

II. *We reflect.*

1. *We explore the texts* (5 minutes). The homilist who is preparing for the next liturgy provides an interpretation of the texts and the specific human condition or experience that the texts address. We don't try to make the readings fit together. Allow the focus of the readings to rise from the texts, not from our effort to tie them together. The participants may raise questions—for which the homilist may or may not have an answer. The object at this point is to hear the questions and concerns of the participants, not to resolve them.

2. *We explore our lives* (5 minutes). The participants share their reflections and insights on what the biblical human condition or experience in the readings has in common with what we experience today. Again, we do not discuss or try to solve problems—either our own or those we observe in our society. We simply offer our reflections as a resource, food for the homilist's nourishment.

(Note: If our homily preparation group does not include children, the adult participants will share their reflections on how the children they know might relate to the human condition in which the biblical text is set. What might the children identify with in the text?)

III. *We respond.*

1. *We celebrate God's love* (5 minutes). The participants share how they feel the readings reveal God's love. In other words, we share how the readings help to flesh out and to clarify the Good News that is the vision of the reign of God. We share in what ways the readings motivate us to give praise and thanks to God.

2. *We share God's love* (5 minutes). The participants share how we can make God's reign of mercy and love happen in our lives today. Again without discussion, we share with each other the challenge of God's word, the tension we feel between the vision of the reign of God and the reality of our lives. What difference does God's word make in our lives, and what are we going to do about it?

(Note: If the group does not include children, participants will want to share how they feel God's word might motivate the children they know. The object is to provide conditions in which the children *freely* conform their lives to God's word. We avoid using the scriptures to moralize or impose a code of conduct on our children.)

3. *We give thanks and praise to God* (3 minutes). We close with a short prayer of gratitude.

This method of exploring God's word with a preparation group puts the homilist in touch with God's self-revelation as it already has taken flesh in the lives of our children and other adults. Moreover, the group provides the homilist with concrete examples of the way our children hear God's word and are willing to conform their lives to God's word. So equipped, the homilist is better able to reflect on the word with either a small assembly of children, in which more interaction can occur, or with a large assembly, in which the homilist takes a more active role in guiding the assembly's reflections and responses to the mystery of God's presence.

Summary

Homiletics is an art. As such, each homilist eventually finds a method and process of preparing that is unique to the individual. Also, as an art, homiletics requires giving of one's self. Such self-giving does not come as a shot from the hip but as a gift from the heart. So, whether or not we follow or vary the method and group process proposed in this chapter, our task as children's homilists requires a personal investment.

• Homiletics requires *prayer*. To pray is to be responsive to the Spirit within us and around us. From our own knowledge of the movement of the Spirit can we speak with sensitivity to the mystery of God's action in our lives.

• Homiletics requires *time*. We need quiet time to read, to reflect, and to stand back from and observe our lives. Each homilist will require different amounts and kinds of time for preparation. If we can schedule even short periods of time regularly through the week, we will find a rhythm to our reflections that is far more effective than a single "cram session." It helps to keep in mind that God is always with us, so while we do need to shut out distractions, we need not go far to prepare.

• Homiletics requires *study*. We have a responsibility to keep ourselves fresh in a variety of areas, including exegetics, biblical theology, the influences of fundamentalism, communications and storytelling, children's literature, children's television, as well as movements in society that influence our children and the way we live. (See *Bibliography & Resources* for a selection of titles related to liturgy, homiletics, and the scriptures.)

• Homiletics requires *structure*. Even though our approach attempts to follow the lead of our children, we do provide a structure within which our children explore God's presence in the word. With either large assemblies of children or small gatherings, the structure helps give clarity and focus to our reflections.

• Homiletics requires *imagination*. This does not mean taking children off on a fantasy to a great Disneyland in the sky. Rather, the successful homilist develops the sensitivity to recognize the simple, biblical images, symbols, and metaphors that make the mystery of God's presence concrete and tangible, here and now.

• Homiletics requires *evaluation*. Sometimes we are not aware of the effect of our style, our use of pet expressions, or repetition of ideas. The feedback of team members can help to keep us fresh and alert. Often our children's response gives us clues—when we are attentive to them.

Clearly, homiletics requires a personal commitment and investment. As servants of God's presence, would we want to give any less?

REFLECTIONS

1. What are for you the highlights of this chapter?

2. How would you describe the attitude with which we might approach forming or participating in a homily preparation group?

3. Read a passage from the scriptures in your group; invite each group member to share their first impressions that the reading made upon them. Note how each person's hearing complemented or differed from the others. Reflect on why the variations occurred or did not occur. What influence did the individual person's experience have upon what was heard? What does our individual experiences reveal of the variety of ways in which God's self-revelation occurs?

4. Reflect with one another on what it means to read the scriptures prayerfully. With what awareness or attitude are we to approach the scriptures in order to read them prayerfully? How does this experience differ from Bible study?

5. If you are in a pre-service or in-service training group, follow the process of personal preparation before meeting with your group. Then, with the group, share

what you experienced in the course of your listening, reflecting and responding to God's word.

6. Reflect on the preparation group process, step by step. At each step discuss with each other these suggested questions: Why is this step significant? How does this step draw me/us into God's word and, thereby, into a deeper personal relationship with God? What in my life is getting in the way of my hearing, reflecting, and responding to God's word? What am I going to do about it?

7. What can you try to do in order to "unclutter" yourself so that you might hear and speak God's word with the simple clarity and wonder of a child?

FOOTNOTES

[1] *Fulfilled in Your Hearing: The Homily in the Sunday Assembly*, The Bishops' Committee on Priestly Life and Ministry, NCCB, © 1982 United States Catholic Conference, Inc., Washington, D.C., p 29.

Chapter Nine

APPLICATION:
THE INQUIRY METHOD

We thank God continually because when you received the word of God . . . you accepted it not as our word, but as it actually is, the word of God, which is at work in you who believe.

1 Thessalonians 2:13

The following sample is for the feast of the Body and Blood of Christ. The readings are from the *SUNDAY Book of Readings* lectionary, endorsed for liturgical use by the Canadian Conference of Catholic Bishops.[1] In keeping with the *Directory for Masses With Children* (Paragraph 43), the authors have elected to use the first reading from Year C because it seems best suited "to the capacity of children."[2] Following the readings, we will consider how a homily might take shape in keeping with the inquiry method.

FIRST READING: *1 Corinthians* 11: 23-26

"Brothers and sisters,
  This is what Jesus did at supper
  the night before he died.
  He took bread, and after he gave thanks,
  he broke the bread and said,

'This is my body, which I am giving for you.
When you eat this bread, remember me.'

"After supper, he took a cup of wine and said,

'This cup is the new covenant in my blood.
When you drink from this cup, remember me.'

"For when you eat this bread
and drink from this cup,
you are proclaiming the death of the Lord
until he comes again."

The Word of the Lord.

RESPONSE: *Psalm* 104
"You are the one who feeds us,
giving us food from your hand.
You are the one who feeds us,
giving us all we need."

GOSPEL ACCLAMATION: *John* 6:35
"I am the Bread of Life," says the Lord.
"All who eat this Bread will live forever.
Alleluia, alleluia!"

GOSPEL: *John* 6:35, 51-56
"Jesus said to the people,

'I am the bread of life.
Anyone who comes to me
will never be hungry,
and anyone who believes in me
will never be thirsty.
I am the living bread
that came down from heaven.
Anyone who eats this bread,
which is my life, will live forever.
This bread gives life to the world.

'Unless you eat this bread
and drink from this cup,
you do not have real life in you.
For I am real food and real drink for you.
Everyone who eats this bread
and drinks from this cup
lives in me and I live in them.
Those who eat this bread
and drink from this cup
have eternal life
and I will raise them up on the last day.' "

The Gospel of the Lord.

Letting Biblical Images Speak for Themselves

The focus of these readings is clearly on the presence of Christ in the Eucharist. Paul writes to the community in Corinth about what he learned from the ritual actions and words of Jesus at the Last Supper. Although the words describing the event differ in the accounts of *Matthew, Mark, Luke,* and *1 Corinthians,* they each convey the same belief that in the sharing of bread and wine Christ is present.

John's gospel further develops the message that when we eat the bread and drink from the cup of Jesus, we share in the very life of Christ. What a wonderful gift! And so available to everyone. Jesus makes sharing in his life as simple as eating ordinary food.

These images, however, carry in their simplicity a profound meaning; bread and wine in the Hebrew culture are symbols of person and life. So does Jesus satisfy our hunger and thirst for life itself. In these concrete ritual symbols we encounter the Word made flesh, ever present and living with us ... and more. To share in the life of Jesus, is to share in his victory over death ... and to live forever.

Because these images are so concrete, they

communicate to children—and adults—of all ages. Each child, whether six or ten or twelve, brings to these images a level of perception and experience that resonates with the ritual event of sharing food. We need not explore or explain to children the difference between "ordinary bread" and the "bread of the Eucharist." Their participation in the ritual experience itself can be enough to communicate the mystery of God's presence in our lives through the Lord, Jesus. No explanation or doctrinal formulation of that truth, as important as it may be, can substitute for this experience. The images speak for themselves. So, too, we can depend upon these concrete images in our homilies to communicate to children of varied ages the real presence of God in the word.

Applying the Inquiry Method

Consider how the inquiry method or structure might serve these readings and draw children into a conversation with God. In other words, how can we explore these biblical images with children in such a way that the images themselves awaken in our children a sense of wonder in the presence of our God?

1. We Listen to God Speak.

The question, "What did you hear?"—or some variation thereof—begins the inquiry. We can enlarge upon this question in the following way.

"Imagine you are one of the disciples with Jesus at the supper table; how do you feel when you hear Jesus say, 'This is my body, which I am giving for you. When you eat this bread, remember me'?"

By asking the question in this way, we invite the children to be participants at the table. Another related question might be: "What do you think Jesus means by what he said to us?"

Another way of phrasing the opening questions—

though not desirable—would be to ask: "What did Jesus
say to the disciples at supper the night before he died?"
This phrasing does not invite the children into the story
as participants; rather, it keeps children at a distance and
risks giving the children the impression that we are
testing them to see if they were listening.

When we ask the "What did you hear?" kind of
question about the gospel, we might appropriately ask:
"What would it be like for you to be eating with Jesus
when he offers you some bread and says, 'I am the living
bread that came down from heaven. Anyone who eats this
bread, which is my life, will live forever. . . . Unless you eat
this bread and drink this cup, you do not have real life in
you.' How do you feel as you take the bread and cup from
his hands?"

"What do you feel when he tells you, 'Everyone who
eats this bread and drinks from this cup lives in me and
I live in them. Those who eat this bread and drink from
this cup have eternal life and I will raise them up on the
last day'?"

Less effective, and lacking in appeal to our children's
imaginations, would be a question such as: "What did
Jesus say happens to those who eat and drink his food?"
The problem with such a question in the liturgical setting
is this: We already know the answer, and our children are
aware that the question has a right and a wrong answer.
Those children who do not know the answer will likely feel
intimidated and left out. That is not an appropriate
liturgical experience. We gather in liturgy to unite,
not divide.

Carefully phrased questions, on the other hand, draw
the children in, make them feel a part of the experience of
Jesus' presence. To such questions there are no right or
wrong answers. We do not know how a child might answer
questions that explore feelings and personal meanings.
However anyone may reply to such questions, everyone
gets the message: You belong. You count. Such questions

respect our children as insiders, and invite our children
not just to repeat back what Jesus said but to consider
what Jesus *means* by what he is saying.

If we are gathered with a large group of children, we
may choose not to invite public responses to our questions.
We can, however, still ask the questions and guide our
children's meditation on the texts. After we have given
the assembly of children a chance to meditate on the
questions, if we have previously met with a preparation
group of children, we can share with the assembly some of
the feelings and thoughts of the children with whom we
prepared. This is not to say we simply pass on to the
assembly what we heard from individual children in the
preparation group. Rather, we rely upon what we heard in
our preparation group in order to guide us in our public
reflections.

When we draw upon the children's responses in the
assembly, we can acknowledge all of the children's
contributions and bring their reflections together into
focus on the Good News these readings reveal: our union
with Jesus and our share in his eternal life.

We can proceed now to the next step in the process.

2. We Reflect on the Reign of God.

At this point, we continue to engage our children's
imaginations as we invite them to reflect on their own
experiences in light of what they heard Jesus say and
explore their sense of Jesus' presence in their lives.

"Jesus wants us to know that he came to give us life
everlasting. He tells us, 'I am the bread of life.' How can
someone be our food?"

We might now explore with our children what sharing
food means to them. "What are some of the things you
notice and feel when you are eating with someone? What
is it like for you to be with someone who continues eating
without offering you anything to eat? What is it about food
that draws us together? Or that can cause us to feel left

out? What might these feelings have to do with what
Jesus is telling us about the food he gives us to eat?

"Sometimes for certain feasts we share special food
such as, for example, birthday cake. How is eating
someone's birthday cake like eating the bread and
drinking the wine of Jesus? When we gather for someone's
birthday, we often recall past birthdays and remember
things that have happened in the birthday person's life.
What are some of the things you remember about Jesus
when you eat his bread and drink from his cup?"

Prompted again by the biblical text, we find more
questions to reflect upon that relate biblical experience to
life today. For example: "Jesus said, 'This bread gives life
to the world.' When we eat the bread of Jesus, how do you
think Jesus gives life to our world? In what ways do you
think Jesus depends upon us to give his life to the world?"

Such questions invite our children to discover for
themselves the relationship between the biblical
experience and their own personal experiences. Again,
with a small gathering of children, the reflection can follow
the lead of the children. If the assembly is large, limiting
interaction between homilist and children, we can draw
upon the experiences of our children in the preparation
group as we take a more active role in exploring the
interplay between the text and our children's experiences.

3. *We Respond to God's Word.*

Our children's responses to these readings can take a
variety of expressions. For example, we might want to
explore with our children how we can be the bread of life
for others. "When we gather at Mass, we do what Jesus
asked us to do; and when we leave Mass, we live as Jesus
lived because it is he who lives in us. As Jesus said,
'Everyone who eats this bread and drinks this cup lives in
me and I live in them.' "

"How might we, in even a small way, live as Jesus lived,
love as he loved, forgive as he forgave?" Our children will

have many specific ideas in response to such a question.
We might invite our children to resolve to do one thing for
someone else so that we might be the bread of friendship
for someone who is lonely, the drink of companionship for
someone who feels deserted.

Aside from, or in addition to, taking specific action to
share the love of Jesus with others, we can simply take
delight with our children in receiving the wonderful gift
Jesus gives us: the bread of life everlasting. Jesus makes
it possible for us to be so much a part of his life that we,
too, will live after we die! Surely this is news worth
celebrating!

Such a response of gratitude and praise might lead us
simply to sing again with our children: "You are the one
who feeds us, giving us food from your hand. You are the
one who feeds us, giving us all we need" (Responsorial
Psalm). Or, "Alleluia, alleluia! All who eat this Bread will
live forever. Alleluia, alleluia!" (Gospel Acclamation.)

Summary

The intent here is not to impose a rigid structure onto
the biblical texts. Rather, we want to follow a fluid process
that encourages our children to interact directly with
God's word rather than with the homilist. Thereby,
several basic qualities of an effective homily are able to
surface:

• God's word is the center of attention, not the homilist.

• Our children's own perceptions and original
experiences of God's presence shape the content of the
homily, not professional biblical commentary and exegesis,
as important as such knowledge is to the homilist as a
servant of the word.

• The language and expressions come from the
original, concrete, biblical imagery of the texts—not from
abstract, doctrinal formulations, as foundational as they
may be.

So may we, as servants of God's word, be in for a
surprise: that it is we ourselves who are being served by
our children in whom God's own Spirit dwells. To walk
with a child . . . is this not the gift of walking in God's own
personal presence?

REFLECTIONS

1. For you, what are the highlights of this chapter?

2. Following the sample outline, have a celebration of
the word with your group. After the experience, reflect
upon what happened.

3. What are some of the differences between questions
that invite us into the scriptures and those that keep us
out? Why is it significant in homiletics to keep our
reflections and questions "open-ended" rather than
"conclusive" (in the sense of controlling)?

4. The children's imaginations provide access to the
mystery of God's presence; explore the way to formulate
questions that appeal to the imagination.

5. As a group, create sample questions (in addition to
those in this chapter) that address what is in our hearts
and what we might have come to think based on our
personal experiences. In other words, formulate questions
to which we may have answers for ourselves but do not
know the answers for someone else. For example, how do
you feel about that? Or, how would you respond if you
were in such a situation? Or, what are your reflections
about that? Formulate such questions for each of the
three steps in the process: we listen, we reflect, we
respond.

6. Select additional sample texts from the scriptures;
follow the inquiry process with each sample text, using the

questions that you formulated. Consider, for example, the
story of Peter walking on water (*Matthew* 14:22-33,
the gospel for the 19th Sunday in Ordinary Time [Year A]).
Or, the gospel from *Mark* 9:2-10 for the feast of the
Transfiguration of the Lord (Year B). Consider, too, a
parable, such as the Good Samaritan from the gospel of
Luke 10:25-37 for the 15th Sunday in Ordinary Time
(Year C).

7. Review the needs of your parish's children related to
their participation in the liturgical assembly. What can
you do to provide services that are to the spiritual
advantage of the children? Explore with your parish
leaders ways in which to recognize children in the way
your parish celebrates the Liturgy of the Word.

*Note: You can benefit from the experience and
information gathered over several years from parishes
throughout the country by calling the children's liturgy
consulting services of Treehaus Communications. Also,
through this service, you can be put in touch with other
parish leaders willing to share their experience and to learn
from your own parish situation. Moreover, you can receive
information on attending or arranging for workshops and
institutes on a variety of subjects, including the spiritual
life of children, homiletics for children, liturgy of the word
with children, the sacraments of initiation for children, and
a variety of other training seminars. Call toll free: (800)
638-4287 between 9 a.m. and 5 p.m. Eastern Time.*

FOOTNOTES

[1] *The SUNDAY Book of Readings.* Christiane Brusselmans, Sr. Paule Freeburg, D.C., Rev. Edward Matthews, Christopher Walker, © 1989, 1992 Forum Katecheticum. Treehaus Communications, Inc. Loveland, Ohio. Year A, pp. 68-69; Year B, pp. 62-63; Year C, pp. 64-65.

[2] *Directory for Masses With Children,* © 1973 United States Conference of Catholic Bishops, Washington, D.C., No. 43.

Appendix

Appendix

WORKING WITH
A TROUBLESOME PASSAGE

This sample provides a scenario of how a homily with children might flow and how you might deal with a translation of a passage that may be troublesome to children. The readings, for the first week of Advent, are taken from the weekday lectionary for Masses with children, approved for experimental use by the U.S. bishops.

FIRST READING: *Isaiah 30:19b-21*

A reading from the book of the prophet Isaiah.

> The Lord God will be gracious to you
> > when he hears your cry.
> The Lord is kind,
> > and as soon as he hears you crying,
> > he will come to help you.
> The Lord has caused you trouble and sorrow
> > by not giving you enough bread and water.
> But now you will see the Lord.
> He is your guide,
> > and he will no longer be hidden from you.
> Whether you turn to the right or to the left,
> > you will hear a voice saying,
> > > "This is the road! Now follow it."

The word of the Lord.

RESPONSORIAL PSALM: *Psalm* 25:4-5abc, 8-9, 10 and 14

R/ (1) To you, O Lord, I lift my soul.

>   Show me your paths and teach me to follow;
>   guide me by your truth and instruct me.
>   You keep me safe.

R/ To you, O Lord, I lift my soul.

>   You are honest and merciful, and you teach sinners
>   how to follow your path.
>   You lead humble people to do what is right
>   and to stay on your path.

R/ To you, O Lord I lift my soul.

>   In everything you do, you are kind and faithful
>   to everyone who keeps our agreement with you.
>   Our Lord, you are the friend of our worshipers,
>   and you make an agreement with all of us.

R/ To you, O Lord, I lift my soul.

GOSPEL ACCLAMATION: *Psalm* 85:8

R/ Alleluia, alleluia.

>   Lord, show us your mercy and love,
>   and grant us your salvation.

R/ Alleluia, alleluia.

GOSPEL: *Luke* 12:35-38 *See that you are prepared.*

A reading from the holy gospel according to Luke.

>   Jesus said to his disciples:
>   "Be ready and keep your lamps burning
>   just like those servants who wait up
>   for their master to return from a wedding feast.
>   As soon as he comes and knocks,
>   they open the door for him.
>   "Servants are fortunate
>   if their master finds them awake and ready
>   when he comes!

I promise you that he will get ready
and have his servants sit down so he can serve them.
Those servants are really fortunate
   if their master finds them ready,
even though he comes late at night
   or early in the morning."
The gospel of the Lord.[1]

Background Reflections

As you reflect upon the first reading, you observe that the prophet Isaiah reminds the Israelites—and us—never to give up hope even when feeling lost. As Isaiah says, God will always remain faithful. God will show us the way. God will seek out all who are lost. God will lead us back to the right path and keep us safe. God is our hope and our salvation.

However, aside from problem of the masculine imagery of God, you wonder: How does the second line from *Isaiah* complement the image of a compassionate God who comes to help us when we cry? As you recall, that line reads: "The Lord has caused you trouble and sorrow by not giving you enough bread and water." What will our children understand Isaiah means? Why would a God who comes to us when we cry *cause you trouble and sorrow by not giving you enough bread and water*? The language is likely to confuse children, particularly those under age 9. So, what do you do?

For younger children, you may decide simply to skip the reading and focus only on the gospel.

For older children, one choice would be: Check several other translations to see in what way we might further adapt the text. For example, today's English Version (also published as the Good News Bible) treats the passage this way: "The Lord will make you go through hard times, but he himself will be there to teach you, and you will not have to search for him any more." This says something quite

different from God *causes* hardship. It suggests that the
hard times are already there and, moreover, God does not
make you go through them alone but goes with you to
guide you through them as a teacher. In a sense, the
popular expression fits: "No pain, no gain."

What about other translations? The Jerusalem Bible
treats the passage this way: "When the Lord has given you
the bread of suffering and the water of distress, he who is
your teacher will hide no longer, and you will see your
teacher with your own eyes." The expression, ". . . the
Lord has given you the bread of suffering," conveys an
image that, again, is nuanced differently than ". . . the
Lord causes you trouble and sorrow." Also, the association
of the image of *bread* with suffering gives a clue that
something good can come from this suffering. In other
words, *bread* is a source of life; so, too, can suffering that is
of God be a source of life.

Bread is a concrete and powerful image; but is this
mixed imagery and its meaning still too subtle for
children? For some, perhaps; for others, maybe not.

Undecided, you check another translation. The
Catholic Study Bible, using the New American Bible
translation, treats the passage this way: "The Lord will
give you the bread you need and the water for which you
thirst. No longer will your Teacher hide himself, but with
your own eyes you shall see your Teacher. . . ."

Obviously, this translation avoids the complex image
entirely. It suggests that in your hunger and thirst you
will find God and learn the ways of God. If you substitute
this translation for the troublesome line, the reading
would be: "The Lord is kind, and as soon as he hears you
crying, he will come to help you. The Lord will give you
the bread you need and the water for which you thirst.
You will see the Lord. He is your guide, and he will no
longer be hidden from you. Whether you turn to the
right or to the left, you will hear a voice saying, 'This
is the road! Now follow it.' " This option is a viable

solution and probably the easiest way out of the problem that the lectionary for children presents.

There is, however, still another choice: simply drop those lines. However, that leaves quite a hole in the reading, though the image of a caring, gracious God remains.

After reviewing options such as these, and perhaps others, let's say you decide to stay with the passage as it appears in the children's lectionary and deal with it. Or, better, you decide—*with the help of the children in the assembly*—to deal with it. After meeting with your homily preparation group, you feel that the idea of finding God's presence in our suffering will be a source of hope to our children in their troubled times. (We will see later how this interpretation might unfold in the homily itself.)

Our thoughts turn now to the gospel. Jesus, in the gospel parable, encourages us to be watchful and he elaborates on what we have to look forward to. Like the servants are watchful for their master to return from the wedding feast, so are we watchful for our Master to return from his heavenly wedding feast.

The servants in the parable are not sure how long they will have to wait. Wedding feasts can carry on until the early hours of the morning. The servants did not take advantage of their master's absence to sleep or fool around and have a party for themselves. Because these servants have hope, they are always ready for their master's coming. And what's more, *the master will return to serve them!* What a switch: servants served by their master! Dare we hope to be treated like this when our Lord returns? But then . . . it's God's word. Who would want to sleep in anticipation of this event? Who would want not to stay awake?

It's God's way.

So do we pray: "To you, O Lord, I lift my soul. Show me your paths . . . and instruct me" (Responsorial Psalm 25).

Reflecting on the Readings With Children

In this scenario, you will find that we move through the three parts of the inquiry process twice; once with the first reading from *Isaiah* and, secondly, with the gospel. The separate treatment of the gospel might be appropriate in an assembly of children from 6 to 9 years old, in which case you might not include the first reading in the celebration. In the case of either readings, the objective is to celebrate the gracious God of Isaiah and the Good News of the God of surprises for whom we wait in joy and hope.

We do not intend to suggest that treating both readings separately as a regular model to follow in structuring homilies. This scenario does show, however, how the three steps of the inquiry process can be repeated more than once in a single homily.

THE FIRST READING

1. *We listen to God speak.*

After the children have listened to both readings in the ritual proclamation of the word, you may want to read again the text from *Isaiah*, stopping after the first sentence: "The Lord is kind, and as soon as he hears you crying, he will come to help you." Invite the children to imagine, silently: What kind of person is it who, when s/he hears me crying, comes to help me?

After the children have reflected quietly for as long as you feel is right, then you might ask if any of the children would care to share their descriptions of this person. Perhaps some of the children will tell you about what happened to them when they were crying and someone came to help them. You need not draw any conclusions, only support the children in their contributions as a composite description of *their* person emerges. The object still at this point is for the children to continue listening in their hearts to what God is saying to us.

You continue by reading the troublesome line: "The Lord has caused you (or allowed you to feel) trouble and sorrow by not giving you enough bread and water. . . ." You pause in wonder, and you invite the children to wonder: "How can it be that this same kind and caring person, who comes to help me when I am crying, causes me "trouble and sorrow by not giving (me) enough bread and water?" Why might this loving person not give me enough bread and water? What do you hear Isaiah telling us about God?

Pause for the children's responses and, drawing from them, you might guide their reflections along these lines: We just heard Isaiah tell us that the Lord hears our cries. Isaiah also wants us to know that the Lord knows how troubled we feel when we don't have what we need—when we are hungry and thirsty, not just for food but for friends and care and comfort.

Do you sometimes wonder: Why do terrible things happen to me? What good can come from my hurting? Let's listen to what Isaiah says about our trouble and sorrow: "Now you will see the Lord. He is your guide, and he will no longer be hidden from you."

2. *We reflect on the reign of God.*

At this point, you might invite the children, again, to share their reflections by focusing on their own experiences of hard times. Drawing upon their reflections, you might focus on the common experience that, often, when we are in need of help, we see more clearly how we need each other and how dependent we are on each other . . . and upon God.

The trouble we experience, that Isaiah describes is of God, can help us to see God even more clearly and to know that *especially* in our suffering, God is with us. Even in our suffering we can come to know God's love and care. Our suffering can give us reason not to despair but to hope in the Lord. So, too, God wants us to know, "whether you

turn to the right or to the left"—no matter where we go—
God will be there to guide us. God is our hope and our
salvation!

So, too, whenever we help one another in times of
trouble, God is present there. We give each other reason
to hope. Then, too, we see clearly the reign of God. We
see God's kingdom come and God's will being done on
earth as it is in heaven.

3. We respond to God's word.

At this point, your focus on the reflections of the
children might lead to a prayerful response: "What a
wonderful person is the Lord our God—who does not hide
from us but walks with us, hears our cries, talks with us,
and shows us the way. So it is right for us to hope in the
Lord, to lift up our souls to the Lord, our God. 'Lord, show
us your path; you are kind and faithful to all who follow
your way.' "

In the same prayerful spirit, you might continue your
reflection by turning now to the gospel.

THE GOSPEL READING

1. We listen to God speak.

In the gospel, Jesus tells us more about following the
way of the Lord and to have hope in the Lord. Let's recall
what Jesus said.

In so doing, you might want to read the gospel again.
Then you might invite the children to imagine: You are
one of the servants of a very wealthy person who owns a
very large and beautiful house. You are happy to be there
because you live there, too. Although you have to work,
you have a beautiful place to live, good food to eat, and you
are safe from harm.

When the owner of the house is gone, you are eager for the owner to return. If something happens to the owner, you may be without work and a place to live. So you sit up with the lights on and wait . . . and wait . . . no matter how tired you may feel. When the owner returns, you quickly open the door and welcome the owner back home again.

But then . . . what happens! Surprise! The owner invites you to sit down and rest because the owner wants to serve you!

You might now explore with the children why they think the owner of the house would serve them after celebrating all evening at a wedding. Wouldn't you think the owner would want to go straight to bed?

2. *We reflect on the reign of God.*

A possible line of reflection: What kind of person—one who is wealthy enough to have servants and who is tired after celebrating a wedding—goes to the trouble of serving refreshments late at night to the hired help? In what way is this person anything like the person who, when hearing our cry, comes to us and helps us? Again, explore with the children their image of this kind of gracious person.

You might draw the children's reflections together again on the way life is when God reigns: full of surprises. The kind of person who serves those who are servants is none other than our Lord, the very same Lord for whom we wait, and long for, and hope to see face to face. This is the Lord who comes to show us mercy and love when we are hungry and thirsty . . . and who invites us to do the same.

3. *We respond to God's word.*

So do we pray in praise and thanksgiving: "To you, O Lord, I lift up my soul. Lord show us your way to be kind and merciful to each other. Teach us your way. To you I lift my soul." (A variation on the Responsorial Psalm and

Gospel Acclamation.) At this point—unless you pray the Creed, incorporating statements of belief drawn from the readings—you might simply continue a prayerful response in such a way as to invite the children to join with you in repeating the Gospel Acclamation. You might integrate the acclamation with the Prayer of the Faithful. After each intention, the assembly responds, "Lord, show us your mercy and love, and grant us your salvation."

(*Note:* For more guidance on the Creed and the Prayer of the Faithful, see the book, *A Child Shall Lead Them: A Guide to Celebrating the Word With Children* listed in the Bibliography & Resources.)

REFLECTIONS

1. What are for you the highlights of this approach to the readings?

2. Explore with the group what each member would do differently in developing a homily based on these texts.

3. Celebrate the word in the way suggested in this outline. After the celebration, examine what kind of reflections surfaced from the gathering in those parts where open-ended questions were asked. How did the individual reflections affect the direction of the homily?

4. Now what would you do differently?

5. Reflect upon the way in which the same homily might take different directions, based upon how the assembly responds. Discuss the ways in which a homilist, without imposing a course of thought upon the children, can stay in focus on the readings while guiding the

children's reflections on God's word and encouraging
the children to take responsibility for sharing their
own reflections and for responding from within their
own hearts.

FOOTNOTES

[1] *Lectionary for Masses With Children/Weekdays.*
Approved for experimental use by the United States
Conference of Catholic Bishops, © 1993 by The Order
of St. Benedict, Inc., Collegeville, Minnesota. Readings
© 1991 by the American Bible Society, New York, N.Y.
Titles of readings and Psalm responses © 1991 by
United States Catholic Conference, Washington, D.C.
English translation of titles of readings, psalm
responses, Alleluia verses © 1992 by International
Committee on English in the Liturgy, Inc.
Washington, D.C. All rights reserved.

Bibliography
&
Resources

Bibliography & Resources

Note: This selection of publications focuses on celebrating the word with children and related disciplines. Although some of the biblical resources listed here are written for use in the classroom or Bible study context, homilists can draw upon and adapt their insights and ideas for use within a liturgical setting. While these materials come from a variety of publishers, many of them are available through Treehaus Communications, Inc. (prices subject to change). The sources of those not available through Treehaus are so marked; should you need further information on any of these materials, please contact the Treehaus consulting service.

Treehaus Communications, Inc.
P.O. Box 249
Loveland, OH 45140
(800) 638-4287
Fax: (513) 683-2882

CIC UPDATE
The Christian Initiation of Children Newsletter
The *CIC UPDATE* Newsletter is published four times a year. Its purpose is to keep readers informed of developments in the Christian initiation of children, particularly as envisioned by the RCIA and the *Directory for Masses With Children*. You can receive *CIC UPDATE* through individual or bulk subscriptions. For complete information contact Treehaus Communications, Inc. (800) 638-4287.

Sharing our Biblical Story
Revised Edition
   Joseph P. Russell has written an idea book for religious
educators and parents that shows how to base Christian
education on the Bible stories that occur in the context of
worship. This book focuses on biblical stories from each of
the three cycles (with variations in readings as they appear
in the lectionaries of different denominations), provides
background material and offers suggestions for emphasis.
346 pp. Morehouse-Barlow/1988 ISBN 0-8192-1425-6 $19.95

Children's Liberation: A Biblical Perspective
   Relatively little has been written about children in the
Bible, especially about the primacy given to them in the
gospel of Jesus. This enlightening volume provides rich
insights into understanding that unless we are as children,
we will not enter the reign of God. By scripture scholar,
Joseph A Grassi.
128 pp. The Liturgical Press/1991 ISBN 0-8146-1964-9 $5.95

The Spiritual Life of Children
   Robert Coles, professor of psychiatry and medical
humanities at Harvard University, has spent 30 years
listening to children around the world and is one of the
most respected contributors of our time to our understanding of the culture of children. In this book, Dr. Coles
shows us children face to face with the idea of God, in
whose presence they seem to be fearless. Children
discourse on the nature of God's wishes, on the devil,
heaven and hell, faith and skepticism. Recommended for
parents as well as parish leaders.
378 pp. Houghton Mifflin/1991 ISBN 0-395-55999-5 $10.95

The Children's God

David Heller, a clinical psychologist, interviewed forty children of four different religious backgrounds (Jewish, Catholic, Baptist, and Hindu) about God. Though he finds some differing views attributable to age, gender, and religious background, he discovers to a surprising degree a common vision of God that cuts across ethnic and religious differences.

151 pp. Univ. of Chicago Press/1986 ISBN 0-226-32636-5 $8.95

The Religious Potential of the Child
Second English Edition

This book describes an experience with children from ages three to six, an experience of adults and children dwelling together in the mystery of God. Author Sofia Cavalletti offers a glimpse into the religious life of the atrium, a specially prepared place for children to live out their silent request: "Help me come closer to God by myself." Preface by Mark Searle.

248 pp. LTP/1992 ISBN 0-929650-67-0 $12.95

The Christian Initiation of Children:
Hope for the Future

Robert D. Duggan and Maureen A. Kelly provide a challenging vision and practical suggestions for restructuring parish religious education practices to complement the implementation of the *Rite of Christian Initiation of Adults*. An excellent description of the convergence of liturgy and catechetics and its ramifications for shaping the future church.

138 pp. Paulist Press/1991 ISBN 0-8091-3258-3 $6.95

Engaging in Transcendence
The Church's Ministry and Covenant with Young Children
Barbara Kimes Myers & William Myers. "This remarkable book pulls together material from child development, religious education, literature, and the authors' experiences as parents and professionals to address the role of the church in the lives of its youngest members" (Nancy E. Curry, Professor, University of Pittsburgh). This book explores the transcending experience that is natural to children and the ramifications of that experience in the use of pre-packaged curriculum materials.
196 pp. The Pilgrim Press/1992 ISBN 0-8298-0932-5 $13.95

Offering the Gospel to Children
Author Gretchen Wolff Pritchard shows how to offer the essence of the gospel imaginatively to children, with practical ideas on children's worship, liturgy, drama, pastoral care, and study of the Bible. "She has given new life to our understanding of worship with children . . . offered a new vision for foundational parish education. . . ." (From the Foreword by John Westerhoff).
239 pp. Cowley/1992 ISBN 1-56101-0650-0 $13.95

Transforming Bible Study With Children
Author Patricia W. VanNess, a curriculum writer, describes a transformational Bible study process that focuses on wonder, imagination, and prayer, rather than on information. While her suggestions about involving children in worship are not appropriate for the Catholic tradition, her approach reflects a particular respect for teachers and children learning together.
126 pp. Abingdon Press/1991 ISBN 0-687-42502-6 $9.95

The Bible: A Child's Playground

Growing interest in celebrating the word with children and in lectionary-based programs makes this a "must-read" book. Authors Gertrude G. and A. Roger Gobbel examine the perplexing question of what is involved in teaching children the Bible. The authors contend that children should have direct access to biblical texts. A. Roger Gobbel is Professor of Communication and Education at Lutheran Theological Seminary, Gettysburg; Gertrude G. Gobbel is head of the Psychology Department at Gettysburg College.
176 pp. Augsburg-Fortress/1986 ISBN 0-8006-1887-4 $9.95

Children in the Assembly of the Church

This is a collection of 5 addresses given at the Notre Dame conference on the place of children in the liturgical assembly. Although one address supporting the practice of separate liturgy of the Word was omitted, this book does invite readers to think critically about many current practices and the need to recognize the spiritual lives of children. Edited by Eleanor Bernstein, CSJ, and John Brooks-Leonard.
101 pp. LTP/1992 ISBN 0-929650-66-2 $8.95

A Child Shall Lead Them
A Guide to Celebrating the Word With Children

This guide is a companion volume to the book *To Walk With A Child*. Celebrating the word with children on Sundays when the parish assembles is a significant development in the liturgical and Christian initiation movements. This guide takes the reader through the entire ritual, step by step, describing the significance of each part of the ritual. By Gerard A. Pottebaum, Sr. Paule Freeburg, D.C., and Joyce Kelleher.
136 pp. Treehaus/1992 ISBN 0-929496-65-5 $9.95

The SUNDAY Book of Readings
A Lectionary for Children
   Endorsed for liturgical use by the Canadian Conference
of Catholic Bishops, this lectionary adapted for children
features: inclusive language, large type, text set in sense
lines, adapted in keeping with the *Directory for Masses
With Children*, handsomely bound for use in celebrations
of the word, and in a size manageable by children. Year A,
B, and C in separate volumes. Developed under the
direction of Christiane Brusselmans with Sr. Paule
Freeburg, D.C., Rev. Edward Matthews, Christopher
Walker.
172 pp. Treehaus/1991-92 ISBN 0-929496-38-8 (Year A);
ISBN 0-929496057-4 (Year B); ISBN 0-929496-91-4 (Year C).
$29.95 each when purchased in a set ($49.95 individually).

*Note: Contact Treehaus for SUNDAY materials available in
Spanish.*

SUNDAY Leader's Weekly Guide
   Each volume covers 52 Sundays and special feasts.
Each celebration features: 1) Focus of the Readings;
2) Ideas for Reflecting on the Readings with Children;
3) the Sunday readings adapted for children; 4) Prayer of
the Day. Also features Background to the Sunday
Readings and Liturgical Seasons as well as Planning &
Evaluation Form.
   Developed under the direction of Christiane
Brusselmans with Sr. Paule Freeburg, D.C., Rev. Edward
Matthews, Christopher Walker.
178 pp. Treehaus/1990-93 ISBN 0-929496-93-0 (Year A);
ISBN 0- 929496-58-2 (Year B); ISBN 0-929496-92-2 (Year
C). $29.95 each when purchased in set of 3. ($49.95
individually.) Contact Treehaus for bulk discounts.

SUNDAY Family Leaflets

These 4-page and 6-page weekly leaflets are for distribution to families after Mass or for use in school. They feature: the Sunday readings adapted for children ages 5 to 12 years; picture-story illustrations of the readings; prayers; and description of biblical people and places. Essential for family involvement and continued reflection on the word at home.

Weekly / Treehaus / Call (800) 638-4287 for bulk rates & discounts.

My SUNDAY Shepherd
Family Leaflets for Young Children

These full-color seasonal leaflets are for families with children 3 to 5 years old. Designed to help the young child take those first steps—hand-in-hand with parents—in celebrating the gospel story on Sunday and responding in praise throughout the week. Set of 8 leaflets and 1 Parent Guide for each of the following seasons: Advent/Christmas; Lent/Easter Sunday; Eastertide/ Pentecost.

Weekly during these seasons / Treehaus / Call (800) 638-4287 for subscription information and bulk discounts.

SUNDAY Scripture Response Posters

A complete series of 53 beautiful posters (17x22 inches), designed to be decorated or colored by leaders, helpers, or families, for use at the celebration of the word. Each poster features the enlarged text of Responses and Gospel Acclamations and a large picture-story illustration of the Sunday scriptures. Especially helpful for younger children. Available for all three cycles, Year A, B, and C.

Weekly / Treehaus / Call (800) 638-4287 for prices and discounts.

How to Celebrate the Word with Children . . . and Why
A Video
    Features a demonstration celebration with commentary
by Father Edward Matthews, one of the primary authors of
the *Directory for Masses With Children.*
30 minutes with guide / Treehaus / 1990 $49.95

How Parishes Are Celebrating the Word With Children
A Training Video
    This training video serves a critical need: training
ministers of the Word. Observe and learn from four
parishes, including Anglo, Hispanic, and African-American,
where children celebrate the word together. A study guide
aids identifying and discussing what is and is not
appropriate practice. Running times: 10, 19, 13, and 9
minutes.
Treehaus / 1993 Rental: $15.00 Purchase: $49.95

SUNDAY: A Basic Celebration Resource
Video
    A video "dictionary" for the SUNDAY *Celebration of the
Word* material, hosted by Christiane Brusselmans and
Gerard A. Pottebaum. Each element of the SUNDAY
Celebration of the Word materials is described, along with
its uses. An important tool for any parish developing
liturgies that respect the spiritual life of children.
21 Minutes / Treehaus / 1990 $19.95

Lectionary for Masses and Other Celebrations
With Children

In 1991 the United States bishops approved a
lectionary for children, a translation by the American Bible
Society (Contemporary English Version-CEV). The
lectionary is more appropriate for children 9 to 12 years
old than for younger children; the language is not
inclusive. Handsomely bound ritual editions and a less
expensive study edition. The ritual edition lectionary is
available in several different volumes:

Sunday (Year A) & Weekday in one volume: $29.95
Sunday (Year B) & Weekday in one volume: $29.95
Sunday (Year C) & Weekday in one volume: $29.95
Sunday only (Year A, B, C in separate volumes): $19.95
Weekday only in one volume: $19.95
Study edition:
Sunday readings (A, B, C,in separate volumes): $9.95
Weekday readings (one volume): $11.95

Weekday Children's Lectionary Leader/Homilist Guide

This guide provides notes for each of the seasonal
readings and a selection of the feasts of saints. These
notes feature: 1) Focus of the Readings; 2) Ideas for
Reflections With Children; 3) Preparation aids; 4) Homily
Outline aids. The guide also suggests optional readings,
taken from the *SUNDAY Book of Readings* adapted for
children, whenever the same scripture sources appear in
both lectionaries. By Jamie Gustafson, Ph.D.
176 pp. Treehaus/1993. 1 copy: $19.95. 3 or more: $9.95 ea.

*Note: The following resources are available from the
publisher as noted with each listing or contact your local
bookstore.*

Guided Meditations for Children
How to Teach Children to Pray Using Scripture
    Jane Reehorst, B.V.M. Using active imagination,
children are led into a gospel scene where they are able to
encounter the Lord Jesus.
96 pp. Wm C. Brown/1986 ISBN 0-697-02201-3 $6.95
    Wm C. Brown Company Publishers
    2460 Kerper Blvd.
    Dubuque, IA 52001
    (319) 588-1451

The Catholic Study Bible
New American Bible
    Donald Senior, General Editor. This study Bible
combines the full text, introductions, and notes of the *New
American Bible* and more than 600 pages of completely
new study materials written by many of the finest Catholic
scholars in the field. A fundamental resource.
Oxford University Press/1990 ISBN 0-19-528389-9 $34.95
    Oxford University Press
    200 Madison Ave.
    New York, NY 10016

Children in the Worshiping Community
    David Ng & Virginia Thomas. A resourceful book
inviting congregations to understand, to learn, to include
children in the total life of the church.
156 pp. John Knox Press/1981 ISBN 0-8042-1688-6 $9.95
    John Knox Press
    Atlanta, Georgia

Worshipful Preaching

Gerard S. Sloyan, author, encourages preachers to review various aspects of preaching from the lectionary readings. He discusses major stumbling blocks in preaching. Although written for the clergy, the lay presider will also find this slim volume helpful.
77 pp. Fortress Press/1984 ISBN 0-8006-1781-9 $3.95
Fortress/Augsburg Press
426 S. Fifth St.
Minneapolis, MN 55415

Fulfilled In Your Hearing
The Homily in the Sunday Assembly

This document is a guideline for homilists, compiled by The Bishops' Committee on Priestly Life and Ministry. Although addressed to Roman Catholic priests, many of the principles apply to lay presiders who are serving as homilists for children.
56 pp. USCC/1982 ISBN 1-55586-850-9 $3.95
Office of Publishing and Promotion Services
United States Catholic Conference
3211 4th Street N.E.
Washington, D.C. 20017-1194

Jesus and the Children
Biblical Resources for Study and Preaching

Hans-Ruedi Weber. A particularly readable and comprehensive exploration of children in the time of Jesus. The author provides enriching reflections on the way Jesus ministered to children and how children share the experience of Jesus. This remarkable study guide comes complete with worksheets, ideas for children's sermons, Sunday night program material.
94 pp. John Knox Press/ISBN 0-8042-1316-X $4.95
John Knox Press
Atlanta, Georgia

Children Belong in Worship
A Guide to the Children's Sermon
    W. Alan Smith, author, presents here recent findings
about the developmental stages of children. He gives a
critical analysis of children's sermons from the standpoint
of these findings. He shows how children's sermons may
be done effectively, making use of lectionary readings in
order to integrate such sermons into the total service.
While not written in the context of the Roman Catholic
tradition, some of the principles and insights will serve
across denominational lines.
    112 pp. CBP Press/1984 ISBN 0-8272-0445-0 $7.95
    CBP Press
    Box 179
    St. Louis, MO 63166

A Call to Witness:
Reflections on the Gospel of Matthew
    Oliver McTernan. In this spirited book, the author
takes a fresh look at the well-loved words of Matthew's
Gospel, showing us how we can relate the gospel story to
our life and the world around us.
Paper, 120 pp. The Liturgical Press $4.95
    The Liturgical Press
    P.O. Box 7500
    Collegeville, MN 56321-7500
    (800) 858-5450 Fax: (612) 363-3299

Celebration of the Word
    Lucien Deiss, C.S.Sp. comments on the richness and
imperfections of the lectionary (ch. 1), considers the
relationship between the celebration of the word and the
celebration of the Covenant (ch. 2), and then comments on
the role of the Responsorial Psalm (ch. 3), the homily

(ch. 4), the Prayer of the Faithful (ch. 5), the participant in the celebration of the word (ch.6), and the objects, places, and rites which make up the ritual environment (ch. 7) of this celebration. Although not written specifically for celebrations with children, this book provides a lucid perspective of the problems and promise of celebrating the word.
Paper, 145 pp. The Liturgical Press $11.95

Days of the Lord

This set of commentaries is an excellent guide to the riches of the church's liturgy. Especially suited for homilists. Seven volumes include:
    Volume 1: Advent, Christmas, Epiphany
    Volume 2: Lent
    Volume 3: Easter Triduum, Easter Season
    Volume 4. Ordinary Time, Year A
    Volume 5: Ordinary Time, Year B
    Volume 6: Ordinary Time, Year C
    Volume 7: Solemnities & Feasts
    The Liturgical Press   Each volume: $17.95

The Collegeville Bible Commentary

The complete text of each biblical book is given, with commentary on the same or facing page. Now available in single booklets or in a two-volume set. (Contact The Liturgical Press for complete information on the individual booklets.)
    Old Testament: $19.95
    New Testament: $14.95
    Old & New Testaments Set: $32.95
    The Liturgical Press

The Gospel Day by Day Through Advent
The Gospel Day by Day Through Lent
The Gospel Day by Day Through Easter

Brian Moore, S.J. These three volume contain reflections on the readings of the liturgical year for these particular seasons. Through the appointed readings for each day's Liturgy of the Word, you will come in contact with those passages which are best seen to illuminate the spirit of each successive stage of the season and to suggest the kind of influence it can have in our daily lives.
The Liturgical Press   Each volume: $5.95

Informal Meditations for Informal People
The Sunday Gospel for the Rest of the Week (Cycle C)

Feruccia Parazzoli (Matthew O'Connell, Translator). In this powerful and poetic book of reflections for the "ordinary" person, we are called to carry the Sunday Gospel with us, with courage and laughter, into all the moments of our week. These reflections will lead us to the discovery that if we only have hope and faith in God and in his word, we need never feel oppressed or lonely or confused again.
120 pp. The Liturgical Press $7.95

WORDsearch Computer Bible

Homilists will find computer technology helpful in comparing translations of the scriptures and in using computerized reference guides. NAVPRESS provides a variety of such software. For complete information contact:

NAVPRESS SOFTWARE
P.O. Box 35006
Colorado Springs, CO 80935
(800) 888-9898